CW01209816

Between
Severn (Sæfern)
and Wye (Wæge)
in the year 1000

Publications by the same author: main titles

HISTORICAL

The Commoners of Dean Forest, 1951

Laws of Dean, 1952

The Free Miners of the Royal Forest of Dean and Hundred of St Briavels, 1953

Royal Forest: A History of Dean's Woods as Producers of Timber, 1966

The Industrial History of Dean, 1971

The Verderers and Forest Laws of Dean, 1971

Coleford: The History of a West Gloucestershire Forest Town, 1983

The Forest of Dean: New History: 1550–1818, 1995

FORESTRY

Practical Forestry for the Agent and Surveyor: Editions: 1962, 1967, 1991

British Trees in Colour, 1973

Alternative Silvicultural Systems to Clear Cutting in Britain: A Review, 1995

Between Severn (Sæfern) and Wye (Wæge) in the Year 1000

A Prelude to the Norman Forest of Dene
In Glowecestscire and Herefordscire

Cyril Hart

SUTTON PUBLISHING

First published in 2000 by
Sutton Publishing Limited · Phoenix Mill
Thrupp · Stroud · Gloucestershire · GL5 2BU

Copyright © Cyril Hart, 2000

All rights reserved. No part of this publication may be reproduced, stored in a retrieval system, or transmitted, in any form, or by any means, electronic, mechanical, photocopying, recording or otherwise, without the prior permission of the publisher and copyright holder.

Cyril Hart has asserted the moral right to be identified as the author of this work.

British Library Cataloguing in Publication Data
A catalogue record for this book is available from the British Library

ISBN 0 7509 2551 5

Typeset in 12/15pt Garamond.
Typesetting and origination by
Sutton Publishing Limited.
Printed in Great Britain by
Bookcraft, Midsomer Norton, Somerset.

To
J. and A.
('WE ARE SEVEN'
Wordsworth 1798)

Contents

	Page
List of Illustrations	ix
List of Maps	xi
Preface	xiii
Author's Acknowledgements	xviii
A PRELUDE TO THE YEAR 1000	1
Offa's Dyke c. AD 784–96	1
Tidenham Manor AD 956	4
THE REGION IN THE YEAR 1000	15
The Relevant Anglo-Saxon Shires and Hundreds	15
Æthelred II, King of England (AD 979–1016)	19
Peasants and Lords	22
Communities	23
Roads, Bridges, Fords, Ports ('Pills'), Ferries, and Streams	26
The Vikings	28
Taxation	30
Population	31
The Influence of Neighbouring Wales	32
Woodlands and Landscape	34
'Waste'	43
Hunting	43
Agriculture	48
Industries and Trades	54
Fisheries	56
Local Knowledge and the Environment	59
Archaeological Remains	65
Christianity in the Region	72
The First Christian Millennium in the Region	76

Contents

SETTLEMENTS BY THE YEAR 1000	81
Settlements, with Main Landholders, Pre-Norman Conquest, 1066	81
Settlements by the Year 1000	87
Settlements subsequent to the Year 1000 or at least neither recorded by that Year nor mentioned in the Domesday Survey of 1086	94
ÆTHELRED II IN LATER LIFE	99
THE NORMAN FOREST OF *DENE*	105
The Norman Conquest of 1066	105
The Norman Domesday Survey of 1086	105
The Introduction of Norman *forest* and Forest Law	108
Naming of the Norman Forest of *Dene c.* 1080	110
Epilogue	110
GLOSSARY	115
BIBLIOGRAPHY	119
INDEX	125
Subjects	125
Place-Names	133
Personal Names	137

List of Illustrations

Fig. 1 Offa's Dyke (A section)
Fig. 2 Part of the Stone Row (*Stanræwe*) west of Stroat (*Stræt*)
Fig. 3 The mighty *Sæfern*
Fig. 4 The meandering *Wæge*
Fig. 5 Silver pennies of Æthelred II
Fig. 6 Anglo-Saxon Warriors and Horsemen
Fig. 7 Anglo-Saxon Warriors
Fig. 8 Anglo-Saxon Sword-armed Warriors
Fig. 9 Woodland work
Fig. 10 Hawking, Falconry
Fig. 11 Deer
Fig. 12 Wild boar
Fig. 13 Agriculture: Ploughing, Cultivating, and Shepherding
Fig. 14 Agriculture: Haymaking, Reaping corn, Domestic swine foraging in Autumn, and Threshing
Fig. 15 'Scowles' – iron-ore workings
Fig. 16 A Group of putchers in *Sæfern* near *Dyddanhamme*
Fig. 17 A Group of salmon putchers in *Sæfern*
Fig. 18 May Hill
Fig. 19 The *Sæfern* tidal bore
Fig. 20 Megaliths etc: (a) The Longstone between Staunton and Coleford
(b) The Broadstone east of Stroat (*Stræt*) alongside (west of) *Sæfern*
(c) The Cwm Stone (perhaps a megalith) at Huntsham alongside *Wæge*
Fig. 21 The promontory hillfort southwest of Symonds Yat Rock
Fig. 22 Rocks: (a) The Buckstone west of Staunton
(b) The Suckstone north of Staunton
(c) The Near Hearkening Rock (a cliff face) north of Staunton

LIST OF MAPS

I   (Frontispiece) The region's relevant parts of Anglo-Saxon two shires and eight hundreds in about the year 1000

II   The lower length of Anglo-Saxon Offa's Dyke, built *c.* AD 784–96

III   The Anglo-Saxon manor of Tidenham (*Dyddanhamme*), *c.* AD 956

IV   Betwixt Anglo-Saxon Lower *Sæfern* and *Wæge*, *c.* AD 956

V   Major archaeological remains betwixt Anglo-Saxon Lower *Sæfern* and *Wæge* in about the year 1000

VI   Settlements betwixt Anglo-Saxon Lower *Sæfern* and *Wæge* by the year 1000

VII   Settlements by 1086 betwixt Norman Lower *Sauerna* and *Waia* (based on Domesday Book)

VIII   Settlements by 1086 betwixt Norman Lower Severn and Wye (based on Domesday Book with mainly modern spellings)

PREFACE

This is a millennium book with two differences. First, it focuses on the late Anglo-Saxon year 1000 as opposed to this 'Year of Grace' 2000. Second, it does not relate to England as a whole but to a relatively small, yet unique and interesting, region betweeen lower Severn and Wye in west Gloucestershire and south Herefordshire – which territory soon after the Norman Conquest in 1066 became known as the Forest of *Dene*.

In March 1999, the 2000 millennium only nine months ahead, I decided that it would be interesting and hopefully worth while to glance back and try to discover what in the year 1000 life was like in the region wherein I have resided and undertaken most of my professional life. The region is the triangular territory, delineated herein by several maps, lying between the lower mighty river Severn (Anglo-Saxon *Sæfern*) on the east, and the meandering river Wye (Anglo-Saxon *Wæge*) on the west, from their confluence in the south near Chepstow and northwards not only to Ross, Newent, and Gloucester, but extending even further into southern Herefordshire.* Both rivers (Map I, Figs. 3 and 4) had a profound influence on the region. Likewise did the Anglo-Saxon towns of *Gleawanceaster* and *Hereford* on its fringe, Worcester to the north, and neighbouring Wales to the west.

The reason why that part of the wooded extensive territory (about 25 per cent) later called the Forest of *Dene* is not mentioned in this book's main title is that in the year 1000 no part of the region was so named. (The term *forest* did not arise in England until the

---

* The extent of the region largely coincides with the territory of the present Forest of Dean District Council.

xiii

Preface

Norman Conquest, and the name *Dene* was first appended *c*. 1080.) Hence in the text the use of the term *forest* prior to 1066 has been avoided; and instead use has been made of such appropriate terms as 'the King's wood' or simply 'woodland'.

Where the relevant eight hundreds are discussed, there is no mention in the text of today's only relevant hundred – that of St Briavels (later almost coterminous with the present Forest of Dean) – because it did not exist by name in the year 1000. (It was created from parts of some of the seven relevant Gloucestershire hundreds and part of the one relevant Herefordshire hundred – Bromsash – probably by 1150 and first recorded by name in 1220.)

When considering my objective, I had some apprehension about the problems involved. I am not a historian, simply a student of woodland, silviculture and associated history; nor an archaeologist, yet profoundly interested in the local archaeological achievements of late local friends including Dr C. Scott-Garrett, MBE, Frank Harris, Arthur Hicks, A.W. Trotter [photographs of them are in my *Archaeology in Dean*, Plates Xa and XIIc], and Norman Bridgewater, along with some successors, among them Ian Standing, Bryan Walters, Alec Pope, Gordon Clissold, and Brian Johns.

For the task, my relevant knowledge would be helpful but limited. I was aware that in the year 1000 the region was substantially wooded (probably some 25 per cent, of which perhaps half may have been timber-sized and half smaller dimension and much more open). Much of the region was substantially farmed. The whole was interspersed by many streams running to either *Sæfern* or *Wæge*. My modest insight into relevant Saxon charters, i.e. pre-1000, arose through valued correspondence with Dr G.B. Grundy of Oxford, and use of his most relevant publications (see my Bibliography). A brief introduction to the origin of the shires of Gloucester and Hereford and of their relevant hundreds had been gained from correspondence during 1947 and 1953 with Miss Helen M. Cam of Cambridge University, later author of, *inter alia, The Hundred and the Hundred Rolls* (1963). H.P.R. Finberg, supervisor for my PhD, was profoundly rewarding; some of his several publications are noted in my Bibliography.

Preface

Despite my limited relevant literary resources noted below,* an attempt has been made to portray the region as it was in the year 1000. During the last ten months I have lived many days in and around that year, and in my mind's eye have frequently wandered around the region! Likewise, King Æthelred 'The Unready' – the ruler of England in and around the year 1000 – has rarely been far from my mind. Early in my research a welcome boost came from my daughter's timely gift of a splendid book relating to Anglo-Saxon England in general, entitled *The Year 1000*, sub-title *What life was like at the turn of the first millennium*, by Robert Lacey and Danny Danziger, 1999. Their highly successful book provides a wealth of contemporary countrywide information. For this I am grateful – not least because the only two relevant books with 'The Year 1000' in their title which I have subsequently perused, that of Richard Erdoes (*AD 1000: Living on the Brink of Apocalypse, 1988*) relates only to France, Germany and Italy; and that of Henri Focillon (*The Year 1000*, translated from the French, 1971) contains little regarding England and nothing of this region. Both books emphasize the

---

* Some relative information had been gleaned during my research for four earlier types of project undertaken throughout several decades: (1) For my MA Thesis 'The Dean Forest Eyre of 1282' (1955). (2) For the following of my books: *The Metes and Bounds of the Forest of Dean and Hundred of St Briavels* (1947); *The Commoners of Dean Forest* (1951); *The Free Miners of the Forest of Dean* (1953); *The Laws of Dean* (1952); *Archaeology in Dean: A Tribute to Dr C. Scott-Garrett, MBE* (1967); *Royal Forest* (1966); *The Industrial History of Dean* (1971); *The Verderers and Forest Laws of Dean* (1971); *The Regard of the Forest of Dene in 1282* (1987); *Coleford: The History of a West Gloucestershire Forest Town* (1983); and *The Forest of Dean: New History:1550–1818* (1995). (3) For my locally wide-ranging papers in the annual *The New Regard*, in particular: '*Aluredestone* of Domesday Book' (1989); 'The Marchership of *Striguil* (Chepstow) and the relationship with the Forest of Dean' (1989); 'Ancient Tidenham and its neighbourhood' (1991); 'Grace Dieu Abbey's Cell at Stowe' (1991); 'The Relationship of Tintern Abbey to the Forest of Dean' (1991); 'The Priories of Alvington and Aylburton of Llanthony by Gloucester' (1991); and 'Ancient Locations' (1999). (4) For 'The Herefordshire portion of the Ancient Forest of Dean' (1946, in *The Transactions of the Woolhope Field Club*); and for 'Boundaries relating to the Forest of Dean' (*The Forester*, a local newspaper, 1987). Most of the sources for the foregoing publications have been deposited in the Gloucestershire Record Office under reference D3921, 'The Cyril Hart Forest of Dean Collection'; other sources, relating to Dean forestry, have been given to Forest Enterprise, Coleford, 'The Cyril Hart Dean Forestry Collection'.

PREFACE

theme of impending doom of the year 999. Documentary sources of life and events in England during the years around AD 1000 are regrettably scarce. For Gloucestershire itself, writings on Anglo-Saxon times have included: Ellis (1879–80), Taylor (1889), Fullbrook-Leggatt (1935), Saville (1984, which includes useful articles by Heighway and others) and, the most relevant for this region, Heighway (1987) and Hare (1992, 1997).

Research for the year 1000 has necessitated a study of countrywide literature of the late Anglo-Saxon period. Also a re-study of Domesday Book 1086 in some depth, chiefly to note its pre-1066 manors and other settlements, with main landholders – in effect its T.R.E. (*Tempore Regis Edwardi*) information. Where there is insufficient knowledge available relating to pre-1066, part informed conjecture has been necessary in trying to glance back to the year 1000 – attempted on pages 81–95.

The apt question of the attitude of the region's inhabitants to the first Christian millennium is addressed on pages 76–7.

The sub-title of the book – *A Prelude to the Norman Forest of Dene* – is fulfilled in the final section of the text. To achieve continuity, brief comments have been made on the post-1000 life of Æthelred ('The Unready'), he died in 1016, followed by brief notes on the reign of Cnut (1016–1035) and of Edward the Confessor (1042–January 1066). Brief information is given of the Norman Conquest in 1066, and of the Conqueror's introduction of the legal term *forest* with its forest law and administration. Then follows a note on the Domesday Survey of 1086, from which my Maps VII and VIII were compiled. Finally, an explanation is given of how the Forest of *Dene* (previously referred to simply as woodland, and later as 'the forest') became so named from *c.* 1080.

This attempt to glance back at the region as it may have been a thousand years ago hopefully provides an acceptable portrayal of the life of its late Anglo-Saxon inhabitants, together with an indication of the landscape and social conditions. The region's future, as the second Christian millennium unfolded and progressed, concerned the remainder of King Æthelred's reign, followed by successive kings.

Preface

The year 1066 witnessed the Norman Conquest and the introduction of *forest* and forest law and administration, as well as many other economic and social changes. In that year, modern English history conventionally began and formed a basis for the following millennium. Its history so far as this region is concerned – at least to 1999 – is substantially documented in my *Royal Forest* and *The Industrial History of Dean* supplemented by other books and papers relating to forest administration, mining, and commoning. Meanwhile, I invite the reader to share the results of my research and conjectures, and I extend a welcome to this region in the year 1000.

C.H.
Chenies
Coleford
Forest of Dean
Gloucestershire
1 January 2000

Author's Acknowledgements

My researches have incurred many debts. The eight maps, and eighteen of the figures, all based on my researches, have been produced respectively by Ian Pope and David Hughes whose splendid help and co-operation are much appreciated. Nine other illustrations – from the Cotton Julius Calendar (*c.* 1020) – have been used with the permission of The British Library: they were redrawn for Robert Lacey and Danny Danziger in their splendid book mentioned in my Preface, who have most generously given permission for me to use them herein as Figures 9, 10, 13 and 14.

Thanks are recorded for use of the texts of the Gloucestershire and Herefordshire folios of Domesday Book, the former edited by John S. Moore, and the latter by Frank and Caroline Thorn, published respectively in 1982 and 1983 by Phillimore, Chichester. Thanks are also given to: the staffs of The Public Record Office, The British Library, Gloucestershire Record Office, Gloucester Public Libraries, Gloucester City Museum and the Dean Heritage Museum; likewise to local friends Ian Standing, Gordon Clissold, Brian Johns, Harry Paar, David Price, Stanley Coates, Keith Walker, and Vernon Daykin, all of whom have helped in one way or another.

I also record my gratitude to Dr Oliver Rackham, Dr Margaret Gelling OBE, Dr Della Hooke, Dr John S. Moore, Carolyn Heighway, Michael Hare, and Timothy Porter – all specialists in their respective historical interests – for reading draft versions of parts of my manuscript, and helping to guide my footsteps within the national scenario – to which I have attempted to add a regional approach by a local detailed study. The responsibility for mistakes is, of course, my own.

A glance at the Bibliography (pp. 119–23) will reveal the profound extent to which the book's national background is based on the publications relating to the late Anglo-Saxon period.

Finally, warm thanks to my publishers, Sutton Publishing, to whom I express my gratitude for their excellent and friendly attention to this book.

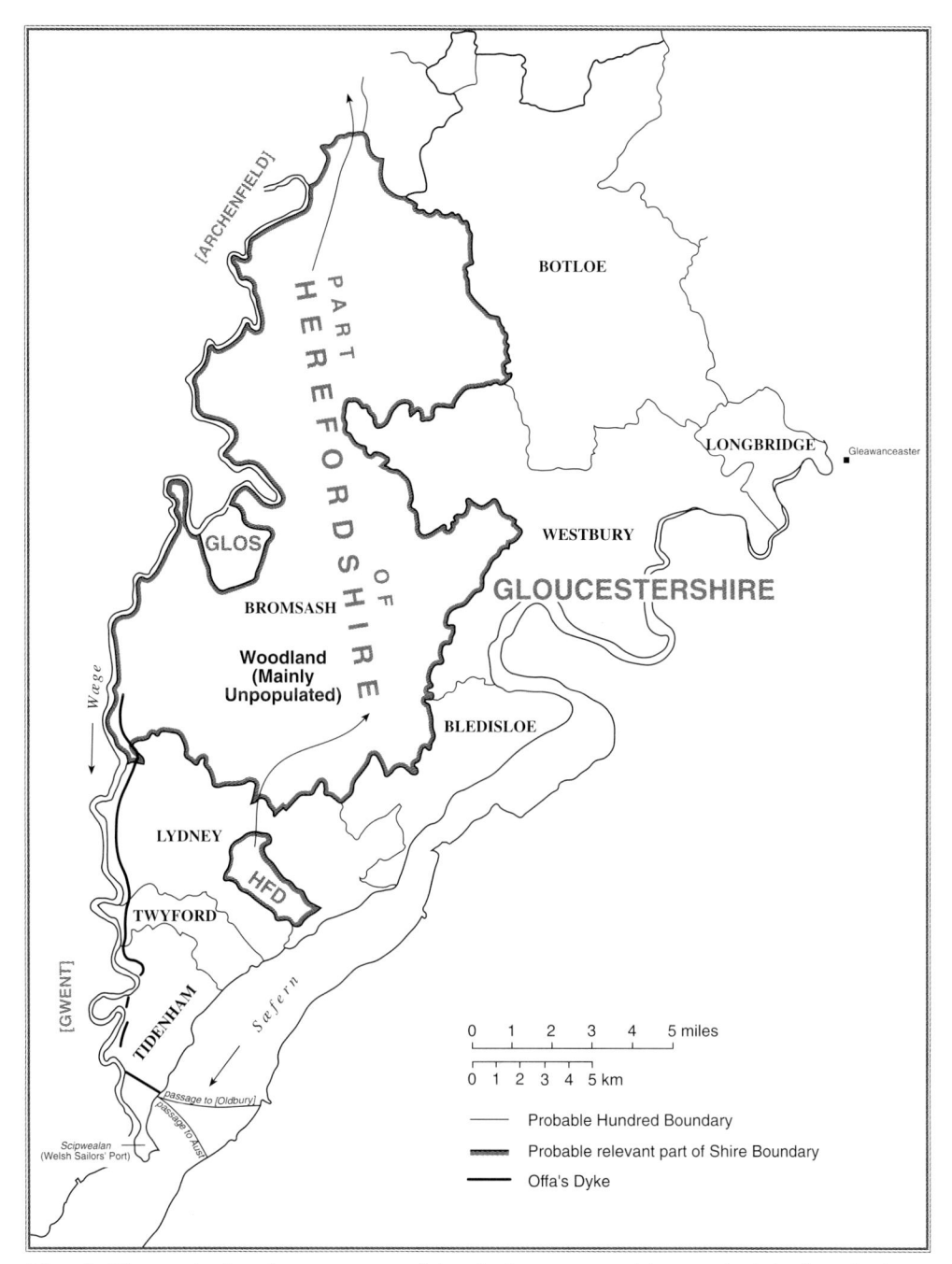

Map I: The region's relevant parts of Anglo-Saxon two shires and eight hundreds in about the year 1000. With modern spellings when the Anglo-Saxon spelling is not known. Place-names in [ ] brackets are to assist location.

A Prelude to the Year 1000

A Prelude to the Year 1000

The history of the region before the year 1000 includes the turmoils of several centuries under divers rulers of various parts of what became England, the influence of the underkingdom of the Magonsætans and the Hwicce of Mercia (Hooke, 1985), and of the ascendancy of the Mercian kings (Lapidge, ed., 1999). Most of the region was under the Magonsætan. Relegating to later pages the many catastrophic raids by Scandinavians and Vikings throughout the country, only two historical aspects will be touched upon herein as being of direct relevant importance as a prelude to the region in the year 1000.

Offa's Dyke *c.* AD 784–96

The extensive earthwork Dyke of King Offa (reigned AD 757–96), with a fragmented part lying in the west of the region, has been called 'the greatest public work of the whole Anglo-Saxon period' (Stenton, 1971). Constructed between AD 784 and 796, it marked the frontier between Mercia and Wales (Map II and Fig. 1). It commences just north of the mouth of the river Wye, *Wæge*, and extends intermittently northwards along its left, east, bank and onwards to the mouth of the Dee (Fox, 1955). Some of the Dyke's history is being questioned, enlightened, or resolved. New information has been found by David Hill (our greatest authority on the Dyke) and Extra-mural students of Manchester University (Campbell, 1991; Gelling, 1992; Hill, 1996; Lapidge, ed., 1999, p. 341).

The Dyke's construction was an act of war or deterrence. It had variable form. At its most dramatic points it had a ditch to the west

BETWEEN SEVERN (SÆFERN) AND WYE (WÆGE)

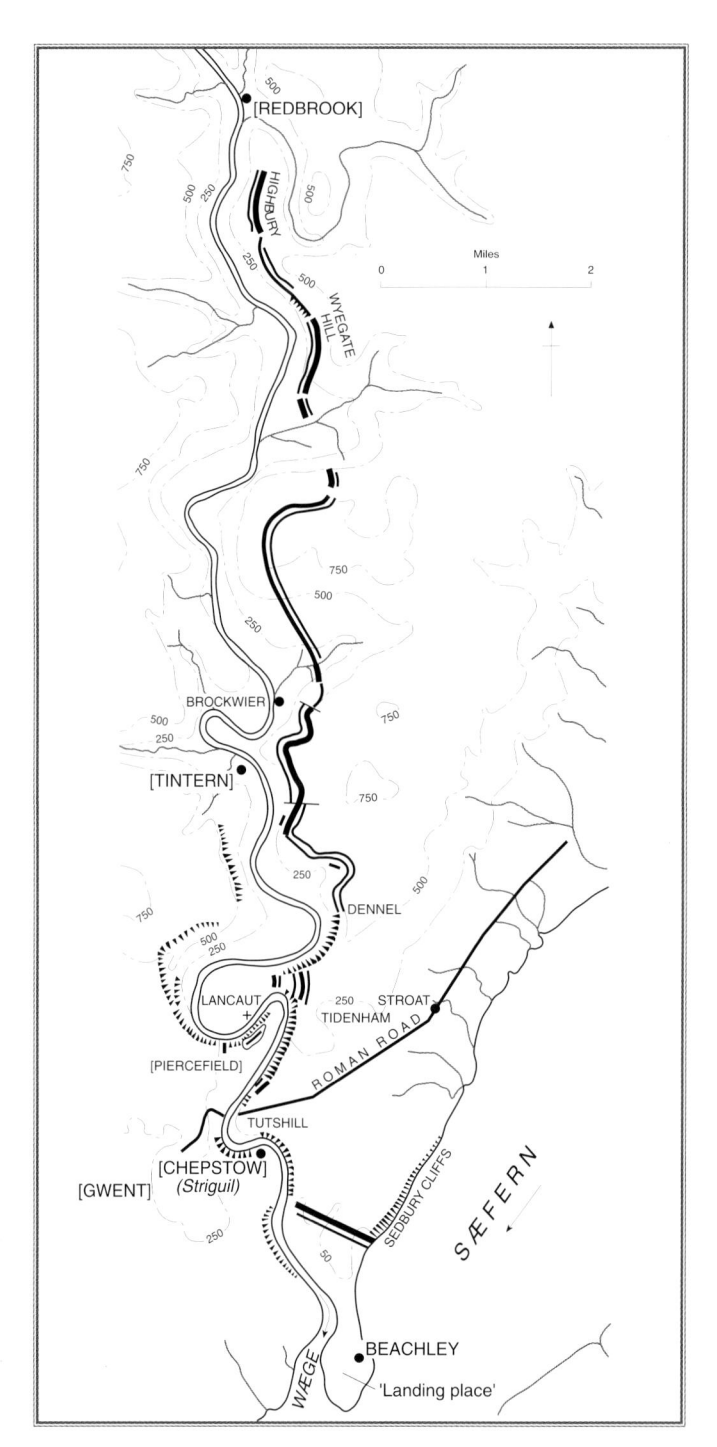

Map II: The lower length of Anglo-Saxon Offa's Dyke built *c.* AD 784–96. Note the Beachley peninsula and Lancaut outside the Dyke. (Mainly after Sir Cyril Fox, *Offa's Dyke*, 1955.) The Dyke would have been well known to and generally respected by the local populace in and around the year 1000.

2

Fig. 1: An impression of Offa's Dyke two centuries after its construction in c. AD 784–96. Throughout its length, the Dyke had different configurations.

about 6 feet (2 m) deep and a rampart rising up to about 25 feet (8 m) above it, the whole structure being about 60 feet (20 m) across (Fig. 1). It was not garrisoned. One purpose was to hinder the theft of livestock: a determined Welsh force could cross it; but their horses would have found it hard to scramble up its high bank, and any cattle they carried off would have found it even harder to scramble down. The Dyke after running, according to terrain and need, down the east bank of *Wæge* cuts across the promontory from Tallards Marsh to Sedbury cliffs alongside *Sæfern*, leaving outside the south point of the triangular terrain (later rented to Welsh sailors: see page 7); Lancaut on the west was also left outside. The Dyke remained of great influence for several centuries, and would have been well known to and generally respected by the local populace in and around the year 1000.*

TIDENHAM MANOR AD 956

In AD 956, forty-four years before the end of the first Christian millennium, an Anglo-Saxon manor in the region is described in the first of three Anglo-Saxon documents which survive only in twelfth-century copies. The manor is *Dyddanhamme* (Tidenham) comprising the wedge-shaped corner of Gloucestershire shut in between the rivers *Wæge* on the west and *Sæfern* on the east, which join and widen into what is now the Bristol Channel; while to the north-east, on the manor's land side, it was bordered by mainly wooded territory (the post-Conquest 1066 Forest of *Dene*). The Roman road from *Gleawanceaster* (Gloucester) to Caerleon-on-Usk – the key to south Wales – passed through it. Across the manor ran the southern length of Offa's Dyke, with Lancaut and Beachley outside it. The terrain was ideal for agriculture, particularly the alluvial soils sweeping to the *Sæfern* on the east; the central plateau land was generally less fertile and more stoney.

Tidenham has always played an important part in the historiography of the manors in England, because it is by far the best-documented pre-Conquest 1066 English estate (Faith, 1994). The survival, copied into the twelfth-century cartulary of Bath Abbey, of a charter of AD 956, a lease of the 1060s, and an undated pre-Conquest survey, all concerning Tidenham, make it a place of exceptional interest (Maps II, III, and IV).

---

* The *c.* AD 930 law-code known as the *Ordinance concerning the Dunsæte* regulated travelling and trade between English and Welsh. This lays down rules for the procedures to be followed when stolen livestock are suspected of being conveyed across a boundary between Welsh and English territory, and for the passage of people from one side to the other. The barrier in question is a river – probably the Wye – not an earthwork – but it is very likely that it conveys an authentic hint of what may have been the regulations along Offa's Dyke (Gelling, 1992).

A PRELUDE TO THE YEAR 1000

Of the three Saxon documents dealing with Tidenham, the first, a charter (Ref. Birch *Cart. Saxonicum*, No. 927; Sawyer, S 610; Kemble, *Codex*, No. 452) records a grant made by King Eadwig to Wulfgar, abbot of St Peter's, Bath, of 30 hides* at *Dyddanhamme* in AD 956. The second document (Ref. Sawyer, S 1555) is a survey which gives an account of (a) the various types of land; and of (b) the customary services due to the 'lord' (the monastery of Bath) from certain classes of the local population, *c.* 1060. [The third, a lease of the manor between 1061 and 1066 (Ref. Birch, No. 925; Sawyer, S 1426), is briefly noted on page 12.] The documents have been studied and commented on by Seebohm (1883), Grundy (1936), Robertson (1956), Sawyer (1968), Finberg (1972), and Faith (1994, 1997).

Tidenham Manor is assumed to have been formed chiefly by clearance of woodland, and had probably been in English hands at some stage in the seventh century. Previously, according to *The Anglo-Saxon Chronicle*, after *Deorham* (Dyrham) battle in AD 577, *Bathum*, *Gleawanceaster*, and *Cirenceaster* (Bath, Gloucester, and Cirencester) had been wrested from the Welsh by Ceawlin, King of the West Saxons (reigned AD 560–91). The manor was conquered in the eighth century by Offa, King of Mercia.

(I) The Saxon charter of AD 956 describes the boundaries of the manor. They ran up *Wæge* (beginning at the mouth) then across by a series of landmarks to *Sæfern* and down to the mouth of *Wæge* again (Grundy, 1936, p. 259):

---

* A hide had no specific measure until after Domesday. It was usually reckoned as 120 acres, but originally was probably the unit of land necessary to support one family – an assessment unit for taxation, rather than a precise area of land. In the Latin of the charters it was described as *cassati* or *manentes* or sometimes *tribularii*. The stated hidage generally affords no more than an approximate estimate of its actual area, because the hidage was probably based on the arable area alone, and the extent of *lēah* (uncultivated pasture-land, and land such as compounds and grazings) varied in different communities. Assessments for Gloucestershire hides have varied from about 30 to about 120 acres (Heighway, 1987). Tiddenham's 30 hides may have been populated by about 30 families, perhaps representing some 250 souls. Lapidge, ed., 1999, pp. 238–9 is a recent summary on hides, by Rosamond Faith.

This synd tha land gemaera to Dyddanhamme: 'These are the bounds of Tidenham':

Of Wægemuthan to Iwes Heafdan: 'From the Mouth of *Wæge* to [probably] the Headland where the Yewtree grows'.

Of etc. on *Stanraewe*: 'From the Headland where the Yewtree grows to the Row of Stones'. Fig. 2. [See Hart, *Archaeology in Dean*, pp. 22, 48 and Plate XIb: 'On the hollow-way running up westward from Stroat'. See also Fox, 1955, pp. 193, 219.]

Of etc. *on Hwitan Heal*: 'From the Row of Stones to White Hollow [perhaps corner]'.

Of etc. *on Iwdene*: 'From the White Hollow [perhaps corner] to the Yew Valley'.

Of etc. on *Bradan Mor*: 'From the Yew Valley to Broad Moor [swampy ground]'.

Fig. 2: Part of the Stone Row [placed stones] west of Stroat (*Stræt*), the northern boundary of the Anglo-Saxon manor of Tidenham *c.* AD 956.

Of etc. on *Twyfyrd*:* 'From Broad Moor [swampy ground] to Double Ford'.
Of etc. on *Aest Ege Pul ut innan Sæfern*: 'From Double Ford to the Pill of the East Island to *Sæfern*'.

The landmarks (boundary-points) in the charter may still be traced on the Ordnance Survey; they are partly indicated on Maps III and IV.

Under the heading *Divisiones et consuetudines* (customs) in *Dyddanhamme* the document then states that 'in *Dyddanhamme* there are 30 hides [made up of] 9 hides of demesne [the lord's] land (*inland*) and 21 hides of *gesette* land occupied [by tenants]. Next stated are the composition of the manor's five hamlets or small dependencies (Robertson, ed., 1956, pp. 204–7, 451–4):

At *Straet* [Stroat alongside the Roman road from Gloucester to Caerleon] there are 12 hides [including] 27 yardlands of rent-paying land (*gafol land*) and 30 basket weirs (*cytweras*) on *Sæfern*.

At *Middletun* [Middleton, Milton], there are 5 hides [including] 14 yardlands of rent-paying land (*gafol land*), 14 basket weirs (*cytweras*) on *Sæfern* and 2 hackle weirs (*hæcweras*) on *Wæge*.

At *Cingestun* [Kingston, now Sedbury] there are 5 hides [including] 13 yardlands of rent-paying land (*gafol land*) and one hide above the dyke [Offa's] is also now rent-paying land (*gafol land*), and what there is outside the enclosed land is still partly in demesne, partly let for rent to the Welsh boatmen or sailors (*Scipwealan*) [who plied up and down *Wæge* and possibly *Sæfern*]. [Here outside the Dyke at Beachley was a little Welsh seaport, discussed later under 'Wales': see Ormerod, 1861, p. 58; Fox, 1955, pp. 217, 280)]. At *Cingestun* there are 21 basket weirs (*cytweras*) on *Sæfern* and 12 on *Wæge*.

At *Bispestun* [Bishton, now represented as a name by Bishton Farm] there are 3 hides and 15 basket weirs (*cytweras*) on *Wæge*.

In *Land Cawet* [Lancaut] there are 3 hides and 2 hackle weirs (*hæcweras*) on *Wæge* and 9 basket weirs (*cytweras*). [Lancaut lay in

---

* *Twyfyrd* later gave its name to a hundred, see page 84.

BETWEEN SEVERN (SÆFERN) AND WYE (WÆGE)

a loop of meandering *Wæge* outside, i.e. west of, Offa's Dyke. The name indicates it had long remained a Welsh settlement.]

The five hamlets may still be traced on the Ordnance Survey; they are partly indicated on Maps III and IV.* The basket weirs and hackle weirs are explained under 'Fisheries' on pages 56–8.

(II) The second Saxon document is an undated but *c.* 1060 copy of a list of the customary services due to the 'lord' – the monastery at Bath – from the inhabitants of the manor of Tidenham (translation by Robertson, 1956, pp. 204–7) [Ref. Sawyer, S 1555]:

> Throughout the whole estate 12 pence is due from every yardland [normal holding of a tenant] and 4 pence as alms. At every weir within the 30 hides every alternate fish belongs to the lord of the manor and every rare fish which is of value – sturgeon or porpoise, herring or sea fish; and no one has the right of selling any fish for money, when the lord is on the estate, without informing him about it.
>
> [continued on p. 10]

---

* Although the extent of Tidenham Manor is stated as 30 hides, of which the demesne comprised 9 hides and the tenants' lands 21 hides, if the hidages of the five individual hamlets are added, the totals are:

	Stated hidage	Yardlands held by tenants
Stroat	12	27
Milton	5	14
Kingston	5	13
Bishton	3	
Lancaut	3	
Beyond the Dyke	1	
Totals	29 hides	54 yardlands [= 13½ hides]

This discrepancy cannot be adequately explained (see *VCH Glouc.*, vol. X, pp. 55, 68). It is suggested that the stated figures (21 + 9 = 30) represent a traditional assessment which is still found a century later both in the lease to Stigand, 1061–5, and in Domesday Book of 1086, whilst the detailed figures for the individual hamlets in AD 956 represent an up-to-date picture of the manor, in which both the lord and the tenants have been expanding the area under the plough.

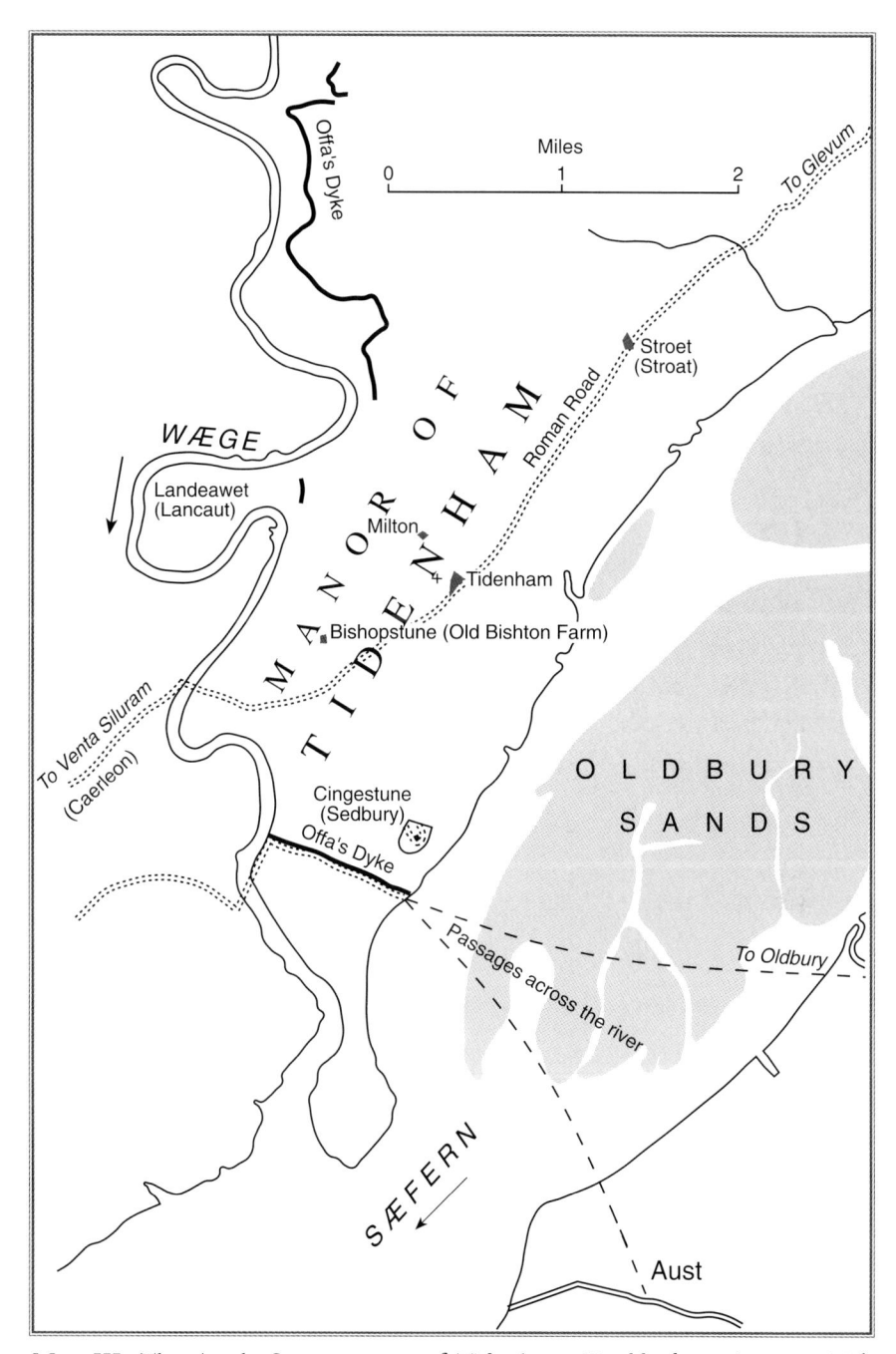

Map III: The Anglo-Saxon manor of Tidenham (*Dyddanhamme*) c. AD 956. (Mainly after F. Seebohm, *The English Village Community*, 1883.)

Between Severn (Sæfern) and Wye (Wæge)

From Tidenham much labour is due. The *geneat* [tenant] must labour either on the estate or off the estate, whichever he is bidden, and ride and furnish carrying service and supply transport and drive herds and do many other things. The *gebur* [tenant, or owner of a yardland] must do what is due from him – he must plough half an acre as week work and himself fetch the seed from his lord's barn, a whole acre, however, for church dues, [supplied with seed] from his own barn. For weir-building [he must supply] 40 larger rods or a fother of small rods, or he shall build 8 yokes for 3 ebb tides, supply 15 poles [measure] of field-fencing or dig 5, fence and dig 1 pole of the manor house hedge, reap an acre and a half and mow half an acre and work at other kinds of work, always in proportion to the work. He shall give 6 pence after Easter [and] half a sester of honey, at Lammas six sesters of malt, at Martinmas a ball of good net yarn. On the same estate it is the rule that he who has 7 swine shall give 3 and thereafter always the tenth, and in spite of this [pay] for the right of having [acorns and beechmast] when there is such mast.

The foregoing information, of which a chief researcher has been Faith (1994, 1997), is some evidence of the Anglo-Saxon land system. It helps to confirm that here was an estate with a village community of dependent peasants who were personally free but were bound to the lord (Seebohm, 1883). The onerous services of the tenants were of a uniform and clearly defined type: they consisted of the combination of two distinct things – fixed *gafol-*payments in money, in kind, or in labour, and the more servile *week-work*. It is fairly evident that this existed in Tidenham from its probable conquest in 577, or soon after, and that it remained Saxon from that time, to and beyond the year 1000.* No other instance

---

* The vignette in Hart, *Coleford*, 1983, pp. 33–4, was based substantially on the Tidenham manor of AD 956.

10

A Prelude to the Year 1000

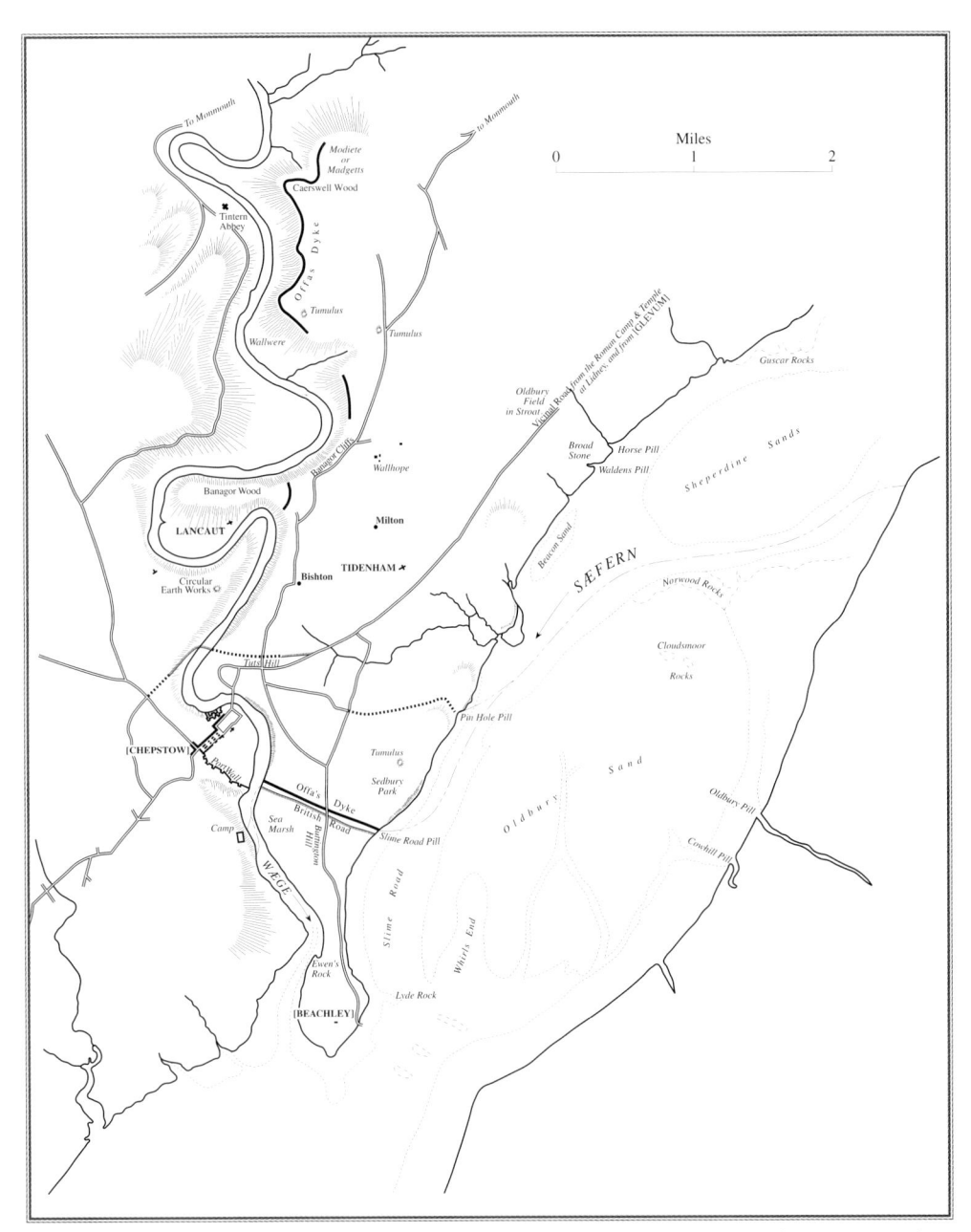

Map IV: Betwixt Anglo-Saxon Lower *Sæfern* and *Wæge*, *c.* AD 956. (Mainly after G. Ormerod, *Strigulensia*, 1861.)

Between Severn (Sæfern) and Wye (Wæge)

has been found in the region of the like character of holdings and services. Other inhabitants of the region would have known what was progressing at Tidenham – with its example of good husbandry and its skilful use of the fisheries in *Sæfern* and *Wæge*.

(III) The third Saxon document, a *c.* 1061–5 copy of a lease from Bath Abbey dealing with Tidenham Manor (Ref. Birch, *op. cit.*; No. 929, Sawyer, S 1426) is not dealt with fully herein as it refers to a situation more than half a century after the year 1000, but its relevance is shown in the footnote.*

It is reasonable to assume that Tidenham Manor's husbandry and life there in general continued with little change as the year 1000 approached.**

---

* The third Saxon document relates to the Bath monastery's leasing at some date between 1061 and 1065 of the 30 hides at *Dyddanhamme* to Archbishop Stigand of Canterbury for his lifetime, subject to certain payments in cash and kind (translation by Robertson, 1956, pp. 216–19, and 469):

> CXVII: Lease [between 1061 and 1065] of land by the Abbot and the Community at Bath to Archbishop Stigand: Here it is declared in the document that Abbot Ælfwig and all the community of Bath have let 30 hides of land at *Dyddanhamme* to Archbishop Stigand for his lifetime in return for 10 gold marks and 20 pounds of silver, and after his death it shall revert to the holy monastery with its produce and its men, entirely and completely as it is then, and in addition 1 gold mark and 6 porpoises and 30,000 herrings [shall be given] annually.

The reference to 30,000 herrings probably implies estuary- or sea-fishing. The witnesses included King Edward The Confessor (reigned 1042–5 January 1066). [The Archbishop forfeited the estate in 1070; it was not returned to Bath Abbey, but was granted to William, Earl of Hereford, d. 1071 (Robertson, 1956, p. 469).]

** By 1086 the manor of Tidenham became a hundred (see Maps I, VII, and VIII) when the hundred name appears as a rubric in *DB Glouc.* f. 164a as possessing woodland measured as 2 leagues long and ½ league wide, a league being one and a half miles (see under 'Woodlands' *infra*). For Tidenham in 1066, 1086, and the thirteenth century, see Faith (1994, 1997).

The Region in the Year 1000

THE REGION IN THE YEAR 1000

THE RELEVANT ANGLO-SAXON SHIRES AND HUNDREDS

The Shires: The division of England into shires during the later Anglo-Saxon period was the most enduring royal achievement of the late tenth and early eleventh century. As early as the Roman period there would have been territories administered by each of the Roman towns, and these territories may have survived to the sixth century AD. The urban territories may have continued to exist even if the cities and towns declined, and subdivisions of the wider area administered by the Anglo-Saxon kingdom of the Hwicce (Heighway, 1984, pp. 225-39; Finberg, ed., 1957, pp. 167-80). Their kingdom seems to have coincided with the medieval diocese of Worcester, and its principal town was also Worcester (Bassett, 1996; Lapidge, ed., 1999, p. 488). Until the eighth century the Hwicce were a quasi-independent political group nominally under the overlordship of Mercia.

The creation of the Anglo-Saxon shires of *Gleawanceaster* and *Hereford* in which this region lay (Map I) – purely artificial territorial units, probably based on the early *burhs*, fortresses – apparently occurred relatively late in the 'shiring' process – in either *c*. 900-980 (Stenton, 1974, p. 337) or *c*. 1008 (Taylor, 1887). More precisely (Heighway, 1987, p. xi) the first 'Gloucestershire' was created in the reign of Edward the Elder or of Æthelred I, in the 900s; it was a smaller unit than the later one, having to the north the smaller shire of Winchcombe. In the reign of Cnut, in 1016 the two shires were combined (Whybra, 1990). Before the shires were created, Gloucestershire formed the southern part of the Anglo-Saxon Kingdom of the Hwicce. The Kingdom did not include the (later named) Forest of *Dene*, but it did include Bath. When Gloucestershire was created, the area west of the Severn was part of Herefordshire (Thorn, 1983, note 4).

Between Severn (Sæfern) and Wye (Wæge)

[By Domesday 1086 the boundary had been pushed to the Wye. Later boundary alterations took place, but on the whole Domesday Gloucestershire remained until 1973, when its southern part became Avon (later 'South Gloucestershire'). Gloucestershire and Herefordshire as used in the text are therefore flexible areas.]

Keynes (1980) notes that Æthelred II (the Unready) encouraged the emergence of the shire-reeve as his representative, apparently in the late tenth and early eleventh century (although it has to be said that the evidence on this point is far from conclusive). The official known as the Sciresman appears in the last decades of the tenth century and is probably the equivalent of the shire-reeve. Previously there would have seemed to be territory administrations dependent on *Gleawanceaster* and *Hereford*; without such subdivisions Offa might not have managed his extensive kingdom so efficiently (Heighway, 1984, p. 225).

The boundary between the two relevant shires from *c.* 1008 to 1086 particularly in the region of 'the Forest' (later the Forest of Dene) is unclear, because the changes that produced the modern boundaries were not made until soon after that year (see reference to the document known as 'Bishop Athelstan's boundary', in Finberg, 1972, pp. 225–7). A helpful discussion is to be found in the latest edition of Domesday Book (*The Gloucestershire Domesday*; Alecto Historical Editions, London, 1987, Introduction, pp. 47, 48). Administration of each shire was by the sheriff, mainly through the bailiff: there was a shire court presided over by the earl and bishop which administered the king's law. Each shire contributed to the military fortifications of the towns of *Gleawanceaster* and *Hereford*; and perhaps to some lesser *burhs*.

Many Gloucestershire places are recorded in the Herefordshire folios of Domesday Book 1086, and some Herefordshire places are recorded in the Gloucestershire folios. The 1086 county boundary differed in several important ways from the modern (pre-1974) county. A detailed reason is given by Moore (1987, pp. 123–4); also in his *Domesday Book Gloucestershire* (1982). The extraordinary situation in regard to *Niware* has been described elsewhere (Hart, *The New Regard*,

No. 15); so too has a like situation in regard to Kingstone, near Weston-under-Penyard (Moore, 1987, pp. 110, 118, 120).

The Hundreds: Shires were subdivided into several hundreds which formed the main administration. Each had its centre ('vill') to which settlements paid rents and other dues and services. The shires varied in size and shape, and formed an increasingly indispensable part of the system of local government. They usually comprised groupings of a hundred householders, more or less. The hundred came into play for taxation, for justice, for settlement of local pleas, and for military defence. The king's clerks kept their records of land tenure and of fiscal obligations under hundred headings. Maintenance of law and order was upheld by regular meetings of the hundred generally held in the open air and attended by local representatives; the local sites are unknown.

The hundred as an administrative division was far less stable than the shire, and their boundaries were often modified (Stenton, 1971, p. 503). [Some changes in the names and composition of hundreds occurred during the reign of Edward the Confessor (1042–January 1066) and some following the Norman Conquest in 1066 as noted in the Domesday survey 1086.] Of the relevant eight hundreds (Map I), Bromsash was in Herefordshire and seven, noted later, were in Gloucestershire, but it is uncertain to what extent delineation of those relevant hundreds had been achieved and were in use by the year 1000. Domesday 1086 names the hundreds as well as the holders of land within them. It also indicates the relevant situation in King Edward's reign – information used later in this text.

The two shires and their eight hundreds would have helped the Kingdom to mobilise either fleet or army, or to pay for fortress, bridge, or road-building, through the system of national assessment based on the hide. They could also collect a national tax, the geld, whose payment was facilitated by ready availability of the silver coinage produced by the numerous mints, Anglo-Saxon *Gleawanceaster* and *Hereford* among them. Whatever the King's desire, a communication to the shires was enough to set the taxation procedure in motion (see 'Taxation' page 30).

Between Severn (Sæfern) and Wye (Wæge)

Fig. 3: The mighty *Sæfern*, the longest river in Britain, had a profound influence on the region. Here the 'S' bend winds near Newnham. The region lies partly to the top (north) and left (west). *Gleawanceaster* (Gloucester) lies east of the top right.

Fig. 4: The meandering *Wæge* had a profound influence on the region. Here it flows downstream in a great loop round Huntsham Hill and Symonds Yat Rock. Part of the region is on the left. On the right, Coppett Hill is not in the region, but hidden behind it the region stretches in great extents, north and eastwards.

The Region in the Year 1000

Æthelred II, King of England (AD 979–1016)

In the year 1000 the Ruler of England was King Æthelred II (he had been on the throne for twenty two years). He was born *c.* AD 968. His father was King Edgar, b. 944; and his mother Ælfthryth, b. *c.* 945. He was crowned 14 April AD 979, when about ten years of age, a month after the murder on 18 March of his half-brother King Edward at Corfe in Dorset (Stenton, 1971, pp. 373, 374). Much that has brought the condemnation of historians on Æthelred may well be due in the last resort to the circumstances under which he became king.

During AD 997 Æthelred's kingdom had been invaded by a substantial army of Vikings prepared to devote a number of consecutive years to a systematic plundering of coastal Wessex (Stenton, 1971, p. 379). Æthelred's dilemma always was whether to fight or pay! In the first year of its operation the Vikings harried Cornwall, Devon, western Somerset, and south Wales. In AD 998 Dorset was ravaged. In AD 999 Kent was raided. In the summer of 1000 the marauders moved to Normandy (where they remained until the campaigning season of the following year.) It is believed that they did not substantially raid within any part of the region by 1000,* but each year must have been one of much local apprehension and foreboding. Huge taxes to the Danes were paid in 991, 994, and 1002. In the summer of 1000, Danish raiders used Norman harbours as their bases (Fletcher, 1989, p. 195).

Æthelred married Ælfgifu of Mercia in about 985, and by the end of the first Christian millennium they had six sons and two daughters: Athelstan (b. *c.* 986), Ecgbert, Edmund (b. 989; later named Edmund II Ironside), Eadwig, Edgar, Edith, Ælfgifu, Wulfhild, a daughter (name not recorded), and a daughter (name

---

* An interesting note is that of a battle in 1016 relating to 'fighting [the Vikings] north of Danaskogar "forest of Danes" (?) at a place named Assandun' (Poole, 1987, pp. 265–98). It is uncertain whether the event had any relation to the north side of what is now the Forest of Dean.

not recorded; but later Abbess of Wherwell). Æthelred, at the age of 32 (by then about 22 years on the throne), along with his wife and children are unlikely to have in any way celebrated the end of the first Christian millennium or the dawn of the second. (See comments on pages 76–7.) Certainly during part of the year 1000 Æthelred was involved in military actions of his own making. He became warlike himself, and displayed 'signs of a strong will and a capacity for vigorous action' (Freeman, 1877, Vol. I, pp. 300–1). In that same year 1000, he had at last got together a fleet and an army; and possibly for the first time he led into battle in person. He plunged into war against Malcolm the under-king of Cumberland, ravaging his territory, and his fleet harrying the Isle of Man. The main cause appears to have been a dispute over non-contribution to Danegeld. Another source asserts that it was the Norse settlement in Cumberland that Æthelred harried (Larson, 1912, pp. 37, 38; but see also Hill, ed., 1978, p. 30). Peace was concluded. Meanwhile, Æthelred had disputes with the Duke of Normandy (resolved in 1002 by his marriage to the Duke's sister, Emma).

Æthelred's coinage played an important role during his reign. His crude image was stamped on the coins, some minted in nearby *Gleawanceaster* and *Hereford*, but frequently made redundant and replaced. They were chiefly thin, smooth, elegant little wafers of silver; notably the silver penny, and the half-circle halfpenny of dull silver alloy. No dates were added (see Fig. 5).

Up to the year 1000, Æthelred and the country benefited in many ways from the resources of the region. He, and subject to permission given by him in one form or another, his family, other relatives, favourites, grantees, lords and the sheriffs of Gloucestershire and Herefordshire, doubtless obtained from the region the meat of deer and wild boar (A-S *Eofor*) as well as furs, skins, hay, leather, timber, fish, and iron items made from locally mined and smelted iron-ore, and possibly sea-coal, the iron goods having been manufactured by the local smiths and forgemen of the time. Probably the nearest he approached to the region was to *Cirenceaster* in 985 and to *Bathum* in

The Region in the Year 1000

(a) Enlarged × 3 sketch. Æthelred II 'Æthelraed rex Anglor[um]'.

(b) Enlarged × 3 sketch. Æthelred II.

(c) Enlarged × 4 sketch. Obverse: Portrait of Æthelred II facing left 'EDELRED REX ANGLO'.

(d) Enlarged × 4 sketch. Reverse: The first 'Long Cross' design of Æthelred II, with inscription usually bearing the name of the moneyer or minter. The cross became used for splitting the little coin into two halves or four quarters, to provide small change.

Fig. 5: Silver pennies of Æthelred II (978–1016). There were no dates.

1009. [The text pages 99–100 refer to Æthelred in later life (he died on 23 April 1016 at the age of 48), and comments on the nickname of 'The Unready' appended, possibly too harshly, in subsequent years.]

PEASANTS AND LORDS

Part of this text is a brief account of the relationship between two kinds of people: on the one hand the peasantry – the men, women, and children who supported themselves by farming, fishing, and a few other skills; on the other hand their lords with powers over them (Faith, 1997).*

The bulk of land at sub-manorial level was *folkland* held by customary conditions. Rent was usually paid both in produce and in military or other services, including bridge work and fortress work. Other than the king, the earls of the kingdom were by far the most prominent group of landholders. Below them were many categories of lords and thegns (Clarke, 1994), with peasants of varied classes under them. The general drift of peasant life in Anglo-Saxon times may have been from freedom (freemen who acknowledged no lord below the king) to greater tenurial dependence on the lord for use of land and his protection. The Danish wars made for the lowering of peasant status owing to payment of Danegeld and taxation for fleet, fortress, and other building. The freedom of free peasants became a community providing either food, rent, or work on the lord's demesne (Stenton, 1971, pp. 470, 472). The development came by way of different classes – *geneat*, *kotsetlan*, and *geburas*, all with different rents and duties, and all overseen by the lord's reeve (*ibid.*, p. 473). The *geneat* formed a class of aristocracy: he was free from 'week-

---

* A recent resumé of peasants, manors and manorial lordship, labour services, and estate management is in Lapidge, ed. (1999, pp. 175, 276, 300, 359), by Rosamond Faith.

work' for the lord, but was expected to undertake certain other duties for him. He paid his lord a rent. The next, lower, class was the *kotsetla* (cottager) who had a small share in the village arable. He paid no rent, but his services to the lord were heavy. The *kotsetlan* were followed by a class of men called *geburas*, each holding a yardland – a quarter-hide (30 acres). In return for his land holding he had an onerous burden of rents and services (*ibid.*, p. 474). Some of the foregoing classes have already been met with when discussing Tidenham Manor.

COMMUNITIES

No Anglo-Saxon major town stood within the region. The two nearest were *Gleawanceaster* in the northeast and *Hereford* in the north – each with its defensive wall or stockade, a market place and a mint. A settlement at Monmouth lay to the west. By the year 1000, some of the habitations which we now know – though small in extent – were settled by the invaders. Presumably, significant numbers of the population remained in their dwellings after raids, and some became assimilated with the invaders. In general those invaders who remained in England proved to be good settlers and farmers. Many intermarriages and other liaisons probably occurred of Britons, Romans, Vikings, and Anglo-Saxons. Within the region the main village was *Dyddanhamme* (Tidenham), with its five hamlets – *Straet* (Stroat), *Middleltun* (Middleton), *Cingestun* (Kingston), *Land Cawet* (Lancaut), and *Bipestun* (Bishton). Other main settlements included *Stanton* (Staunton), *Brocote* (Lower Redbrook on Wye), Alvington, Awre, *Dene*, Westbury [on-Severn], Churcham, Highnam, [Long]Hope, Huntley, *Bicanofre* ([English] Bicknor), Lydney and Newnham.

Tidenham – noted above – was an Anglo-Saxon *hamm* (a topographical derivation) – an estate of a lord with a village community of dependent peasants. Manors varied in size and situations, from vast holdings to tiny farmsteads (Seebohm, 1883, p. 459). The term manor did not arise until after the Norman Conquest,* but historians have earlier used the term for Tidenham. Other manor houses may have existed in the region but far fewer than in other parts of the two shires. Some chief dwellings probably occupied or stood nearby the sites of derelict Roman dwellings, their construction having made use of the Roman local infrastructure and remnant materials.

The population generally dwelt in small communities: either in buildings of perhaps one to four, or a few dozen mainly wooden modest houses, clustered together. Sometimes they dwelt more orderly, circling a small 'green', or extending up and down a single winding road, perhaps muddy or roughly stoned. A priority in site choice was where a living could be obtained – potentially fertile easily cultivatable land, with access to drinking water (there were springs, but no reference to early local wells has been found). Other attractive features were a crossroad, valley, plain, or stream, especially if it had a ford – as in later centuries was the reason for settlements at Coleford and Cinderford (with Ruspidge). Occasionally settlements may have been surrounded by or attached to one or more cultivated open-fields divided into strip holdings, sometimes separated by balks of unploughed turf (Taylor, 1981; Hall, 1981; Hooke, 1981).** The only enclosures or compounds were parcels of rough pasture land to contain cattle, sheep, pigs, goats, and poultry, where the settlement livestock grazed together. Where the arable cultivation was organized

---

* Estates were described by the vague term *manerium* or *mansio* in the Norman Domesday Survey 1086. Before the end of the tenth century, and therefore probably in use in the year 1000, the phrase *heafod botl* ('chief dwelling') was being used to mean not only the house of a lord, but also the adjacent lands which contributed towards his maintenance (Stenton, 1971, pp. 480, 481.) The manor varied almost indefinitely, in regard to size, structure, and internal economy. Some of them covered an appreciable part of a shire and included a large number of dependent villages or hamlets and farms; others consisted of a few yardlands supporting lords distinguished by rank alone from the peasantry around them. In the year 1000 each manor, under whatever term, had its lord either resident or represented by a reeve (manager).

** A recent resumé of field systems is in Lapidge, ed., 1999, p. 183, by T. Williamson.

on a communal basis, each unit of ploughland took the form of a long and comparatively narrow strip. Where the settlement formed part of a manor, the main dwelling would be that of the resident lord or his representative. There were probably some small settlements which were not part of manors. The dwellings, also probably the cultivated arable, had some degree of protective fencing – few planted thorn hedges or stone walls, but probably stretches of wattle or bar hurdling or simply thorn brushwood. A simple community rota for guardianship may have existed, applying particularly to night time.

Social theory in the year 1000 divided the community into those who worked (the peasants, traders and craftsman) and those who fought and administered justice (the king and the lords), and those who prayed – the monks in monasteries and the very occasional priest with his pastoral duties of care to the laity (Lacey and Danziger, 1999, p. 103). The whole region was the domain, predominantly, of villagers and cottagers.

A villager was bound to labour on his lord's land; receiving in return protection of his holding – a yardland or half-yardland, half a hide, or even a hide itself. The cottager had a smaller holding, and perhaps more duty commitments to his lord. The allegiance to the lord benefited the peasants by his protection of their land and livelihood; a relationship that may have involved an element of mutual respect. Peasants with modest size land could well have had a trade as well.

There was some reliance on a class of worker who can only be described as serf, equivalent in status to slave, but there is no way of qualifying how many. Separate was the local smith or the forgeman with his bellows, his duty being to make or repair the ploughs, tools and other equipment, probably serving several neighbouring settlements. Likewise, the tanner, preparing and using oak tanbark to process cattle hides into leather. The weaver, carpenter, and so on would be other appreciated members of the community. As a useful part-time venture, some peasants erected and managed bee-hives, there being a constant need for honey, a precious commodity being the sole sweetener at that time.

ROADS, BRIDGES, FORDS, PORTS ('PILLS'), FERRIES AND STREAMS

From ancient times, trackways ran through and around the region; some formed local and long-distance networks, but their alignment and form are uncertain. Anglo-Saxon *Gleawanceaster* lying to the northeast of the region was connected by one-time splendid Roman roads to more distant *Cirenceaster* and *Bathum*. Lower specification Roman roads ran to *Hereford* in the northwest, including a branch serving *Ariconium* (NNE of Weston-under-Penyard) a renowned Roman iron-industry town (Map V; Gelling, 1992); another branch ran to Monmouth across *Wæge* in the west giving some access to south Wales. To the south, a Roman road from *Gleawanceaster* ran along the west bank of *Sæfern* and crossed *Wæge*, proceeding on to Caerleon-on-Usk (Maps II, III, IV, V). In several other parts of the region lay many sub-standard Roman roads, deteriorating in condition and utility through lack of maintenance and being progressively submerged by uncontrolled growth of trees and other vegetation (Hart, *Archaeology in Dean*, pp. 33–41). Bridge and road maintenance was vital to the road network: the economy frequently demanded the transport of essential commodities over considerable distances. Substantial bridges across the region's two major rivers were few and far between. A Roman wooden bridge later known as *Striguil* once lay across *Wæge* north of its mouth. Another may have spanned *Sæfern* in the south of *Gleawanceaster*; and perhaps a third spanned *Wæge* at *Hereford*; and probably a fourth at Monmouth (Fox, 1955, pp. 220, 221, Fig. 94). There were probably many small wooden or stone bridges across streams. From ancient time a ford (of stones), or perhaps a primitive small bridge, lay across the Newerne stream at Cannop, linking the east to the west in the main central wooded territory. Other fords crossed the streams which later attracted the settlements of Coleford and Cinderford (with Ruspidge). An early ferry route connected Newnham to Arlingham on the east across *Sæfern*. The

The Region in the Year 1000

two sea-passages from Beachley across *Sæfern* to Oldbury and Aust are indicated on Maps I and II. (One later became known as the 'Old Passage'.) There were no ports, but a few places termed 'pills' (meaning tidal creek, which may have served as 'landing places') on the west of *Sæfern*. The foregoing communication facilities and routes were well known by the region's Anglo-Saxon population in the year 1000. The more substantial streams of the region, probably as yet not powering any water-mills, were (using mostly modern place-names):

(a) Tributaries of *Sæfern*:

- southwards from *Niware*, via Cannop (as Newerne), Parkend, and Whitecroft to Lydney
- southeastwards from the plateau to *Twyford*; also from Alvington to the Cone
- southeastwards from Cinderford, via Ruspidge and Soudley to Blakeney
- southeastwards from the plateau to *Aluredestone*
- southeastwards from Longhope via Blaisdon and Flaxley to Elton

(b) Tributaries of *Wæge*:

- westwards from Stowe via Mork ⎫
- westwards from Bearse via Mork ⎭ to Bigsweir
- westwards from Hewelsfield to Brockweir
- westwards from Coleford, via Newland and Clearwell ⎫
- westwards from Staunton via Upper Redbrook ⎭ to Lower Redbrook on Wye (*Brocote*)
- westwards from Ruardean to Bishopswood
- northwards from Staunton via 'Whippington' brook
- northwards from Brierley and Mirystock to Lydbrook
- northwards from Joyford, via English Bicknor to Lydbrook

THE VIKINGS

From *c.* 800 to *c.* 900, the kingdoms of England were constantly kept occupied with the expected or actual Scandinavian invasions, although usually they occurred away from this region (Campbell, ed., 1991, p. 151). Early in the tenth century, the kingdoms came together as England. From *c.* 980 to 1066, England was almost at the mercy of Denmark – the Vikings. The fundamental rule of warfare opposition around the year 1000 was to avoid battle whenever possible (Lacey and Danziger, 1999, p. 154). A description of an example of one of a succession of raids by Danes, is that of the Battle of Maldon in Essex, AD 991, in a great poem (Ashdown, 1930, pp. 23–37; Campbell, ed., 1991, pp. 195, 198; Lapidge, ed., 1999, p. 55). A comprehensive treatment of relevant military matters is given by Hollister (1962); Harrison and Embleton (1993); Hill (ed., 1978, pp. 81–103); and Lapidge (ed., 1999, pp. 45, 47).

The frequent invasions first by Scandinavians and later by Vikings had a profound influence on the history and lifestyle of what became England. They arrived particularly in their well-known longships, supported by their knowledge of sails and rigging and their navigational skills. Their raids were made precisely to demand and by force obtain gold, silver, and jewels – notably to be found in religious houses. As there were none of substance of the latter as yet* within this region – the nearest being in *Gleawanceaster* and *Hereford* and possibly Berkeley – the ravages and effects locally were relatively small, nevertheless the inhabitants were generally kept in a state of apprehension and foreboding. Almost each time raids occurred in England the region's local populace, in addition to paying *geld*, was compelled to contribute men, arms and equipment, and probably food and drink, by Æthelred's order addressed usually to the local lord or the

---

* As to a possible incident in the year 1016, see footnote on page 19.

The Region in the Year 1000

Fig. 6: Anglo-Saxon Warriors and Horsemen. (Re-drawn sketches from Harl. MS. 603 in The British Library.)

Fig. 7: Anglo-Saxon Warriors. (Re-drawn sketch from a MS in The British Library.)

sheriff. A similar situation arose when the king made military forays across his frontier with Wales.

The Vikings' closest approaches to this region beyond that to *Gleawanceaster* in 877–8 were probably temporary landings on the west bank of *Sæfern*. In the channel formed by the two main rivers lie the small islands of *Flatholm* and *Steepholm*, perhaps named by the Vikings or Norse, *holm* being an island. Denny Island opposite

Fig. 8: Two eleventh-century Anglo-Saxon sword-armed warriors. The female on the left is ordering a horn player to sound the signal for attack. (Re-drawn sketch from MS Cotton Cleopatra C. VIII. in The British Library.)

Avonmouth is the only place-name near this region that may relate to Danes, but part is a Saxon word *eye*, an island. Other local place-names along west *Sæfern* which may have a Viking origin include Guscar Rocks (*scar*, a rock). *Nass* opposite Sharpness is derived from OE *ness*, a headland. *Awre* is named from OE *afor-ēg*, probably 'sour island'.

TAXATION

Under Æthelred the national economy rested in the main on the taxable capacity of the peasant's land holding, strained according to time by the need of money above all for the Danegeld given to victorious Vikings, for the building of a fleet, and the payment of Danish crews in English service. Taxation also continued for fortress, road, and bridge-building. Dues were also payable to monasteries and churches. Under the kingdom's burden the position of the individual peasant landowner or farmer must have rapidly become more and more precarious. Æthelred in the face of

Danish raids usually either attempted to fight the marauders or was forced to pay large taxes (Danegeld) to the enemy. In the latter case he levied on his subjects a charge, usually based on each hide, but originally on 'land for one family'. Five hides were usually taken as a unit of liability for military service. In some cases the *geld* was collected through the hundred by the sheriff; it was efficiently levied and the collectors or exactors possessed lists of landholders and the rating, or hidage, of their estate.

POPULATION

The bulk of this region's rural population in the year 1000 comprised three main categories – villeins, slaves and bordars; in addition were miscellaneous categories including tradesmen. Lacey and Danziger (1999, p. 11) refer to England's population in that year as at least a million, and (p. 40) to a total English population of a little more than a million. About 5–7 per cent of England's people were living in towns. Welch (1992, p. 120) and Campbell (ed., 1991, p. 226) estimate the population in 1086 as two million. In summary, England's population in the year 1000 was perhaps in the order of 1¼–1½ millions. Sawyer (1998, p. 150) emphasizes the uncertainties of such estimates.

Estimates of population in Gloucestershire in 1086 made by Darby and Terrett (eds., 1954, pp. 16–19), and Taylor (1889, p. 332), are not comparable: detailed accuracy rarely belongs to a count of Domesday population. Darby and Terrett (*ibid.*) suggest that the recorded population by shires and hundreds for 1086 needs to be multiplied by a factor of 4, or 5 – in order to calculate a more likely population in that year. Their count (p. 191) of the recorded rural population in Gloucestershire in 1086 is 8,280; when multiplied, this might be around 40,000, of which this region might be 5,000. Their count (p. 73) for Herefordshire is 4,545; when multiplied, this might be around 20,000, of which this region might be 2,000. Hence the total for the whole region in the year 1086 might be 7,000. It is difficult to conjecture what lower figure for the region might be applicable to the year 1000; perhaps around 5,000. In the region (i.e. part Gloucestershire and part Herefordshire) in 1086 there were about 500 villagers, tenants and slaves, to which might be added 200 miscellaneous including traders, a total of 700; assuming an average household of five souls, the total population for the region would be around 3,500, and this number, adjusted to the year 1000, might be around 2,500. However, these conjectures are based on a concept of steady growth, not necessarily appropriate for this period. We may never know how near to accuracy the foregoing estimates are. [The current population of the region is about 75,000.]

THE INFLUENCE OF NEIGHBOURING WALES

South-east Wales lying to the west across *Wæge* from the lower portion of the region imposed substantial influence upon it. That is so even from the time when Tidenham manor in the south lay alongside south-east Wales (Seebohm, *op. cit.*, p. 182). The district of *Gwent* seems to have remained in the hands of the Welsh until conquered by Earl Harold from the Welsh King Gruffydd, a few years only before the Norman Conquest in 1066 (*ibid.*, p. 192). To the west of the upper portion of the region lay Anglo-Saxon *Archenfield* (*Ergying* in Welsh, *Ircingafeld* in Old English), between *Wæge*, the Monnow and the Worm (Gelling, 1992), which likewise remained Welsh till Harold's conquest. The land tenures and customs in Wales were different to those in Tidenham (Jones, 1981).

The disputed borderland between England and Wales witnessed only a few battles and other engagements across the frontier during the period AD 760–96 (Stenton, 1971, pp. 230, 573). There were long periods of peace and on occasion even semblances of co-operation (*ibid.*, pp. 330, 340, 342). Much of the quietude may have been due to the warning effect of Offa's Dyke. Possibly there was much inter-trading at selected convenient venues across *Wæge*.* Probably there were some inter-marriages and other liaisons.

Some 'slaves' (an inconclusive term) may have emanated from Wales. Lacey and Danziger (1999, p. 46) stated that 'in England, the Anglo-Saxons proved to be slavers . . . *Weallus*, or Welshman was an Old English word – which showed where the Anglo-Saxons got their slaves.' Much debate ensues as to the differences of slave (Old English *wealh*) and serf (Lapidge, ed., 1999, p. 423).

An important instance of co-operation between the region and south-east Wales was that existing in the manor of Tidenham in AD 956 (noted earlier under the Saxon charter of that year). Within the manor, yet outside Offa's Dyke, was part of a peninsula let to Welsh sailors as a little seaport or landing place, paying rent: they plied up and down *Wæge*. The Welshmen were under English control (Fox, 1995, pp. 217, 218, 280, 281). It implies Welsh control of the ferry-crossing of *Sæfern* estuary from Aust to Beachley (Map II) (the later name was the 'Old Passage') which was the direct route from the west of England into south-east Wales. Likewise it implies that *Wæge* traffic – including a modest timber trade – was important in the tenth century (confirmed in *Domesday Glouc.*, f. 162a, which records payments from 'the ships going into the woodland'). Fox (1955, p. 218) suggests that this part of Offa's frontier may have been the result of negotiations, a treaty between Welsh and English, to enable the former to have untrammelled use of *Wæge* trade and their little seaport; it removed some friction for Offa and his successors, and the English benefited from tolls of *Sæfern* ferry and *Wæge* traffic, as well as the valuable salmon and other fisheries on both rivers.

Another element of the influence of neighbouring Wales is the place-name evidence for continuity of a partly Welsh population in the region (there were probably inter-marriages and other liaisons). Smith (1964) notes: Corse (from Old Welsh *cors*, marsh); Morwent in

---

* The *c.* AD 930 law-code known as the *Ordinance covering the Dunsæte* regulated travelling and trade between English and Welsh (see page 4).

Hartpury (from OW *mor venta*, great market); Maismore (from OW *maes mawr*, great field); Dymock (from OW *dyn moch*, swine fort); Newent (from OW *noviant*, new place); and Castiard in Flaxley (from OW *castein iarth*, chestnut hill). There are also names incorporating both Welsh and English elements, such as Pauntley (from OW *pant* and OE *lēah*, clearing in the valley); and Mailscot Wood in English Bicknor (from OW *Mael coed*, Mael's Wood). Finally, Walsons in St Briavels and Walseston in Tidenham derive from OE *Walestun*, Welshman's farm, and *Welisctun*, Welsh farm, again indicating (possibly with Welshbury) the survival of a recognisably Welsh element in the region's population. The foregoing field of etymology might repay further study (Gelling, 1984).

WOODLANDS AND LANDSCAPE

Woodlands from time immemorial had a profound influence in the region. Dense woods may have been avoided by man as dangerous and unpleasant, but often they were a refuge from snow, ice, wind, and storm, also a source of meat, fruits, and nuts, as well as other products of great utility. The less dense parts were used to live near and hunt in, and from where to take deer and wild boar, as well as wood for dwellings, fencing and fuel (Hart, *Royal Forest*, p. 19). Stretches of woodland were cleared by felling and burning to provide for arable cultivation on land enriched by humus. In the autumn domestic swine fattened themselves on acorns and beechmast, and cattle, horses, sheep, and goats browsed the underwood and grazed the natural and induced clearings.

The country many millennia earlier – at least after the last Ice Age some 10,000 to 12,000 years ago – was well wooded, but Neolithic Britons had started as early as 5000 BC to fell and grub up woodland and produce arable crops – a process which followed right up to the Roman invasion. Roman Britain, in general, did not comprise boundless wildwoods surrounding precarious clearings of the best land; settlement abutted on settlement (Rackham, 1986, pp. 74, 75). The country probably had two types of terrain: regions where there was a patchwork of woodland and farmland, and regions where all the woodland had disappeared. The Romans, aware of the value of woodlands, needed to conserve this limited resource of timber, a habitat for game and provision of other utilities. Still, they became major cultivators of woodland and wood-pasture, laying down villages and farms as well as roads across the countryside. Despite the post-Roman recession, the same situation probably continued throughout the Dark Ages and certainly in the Anglo-Saxon period. Tree-fellers, burners, and grubbers-up of tree stumps, followed by increasingly proficient ploughs, rapidly continued the process. In effect, much of England in the year 1000 consisted of farmlands with islands of woodland. Even the larger extents of woodlands were not wholly uninhabited. Rackham (1986, p. 77) reckons that England in 1086 was about 15 per cent woodland; his estimates by counties (p. 78) are noted later. All attempts to map early woodland are conjectural. Sylvan cover might fluctuate according to the extent to which it was grazed (Wickham, 1990).

A Worcester Charter of AD 866 (Wickham, 1990, p. 507) differentiates between woodland for swine-pasture, poles (*virgis bovis*), firewood (*lignaria . . . ad ignem*), building timber (*materias*), and felled logs. Here a distinction is being made above all between timber (for building) and underwood or coppice; the latter being tree stumps (stools) left to send up shoots which are cut at regular short intervals (rotations) for fencing, wattling, firewood, tools, some furniture, farm equipment, and other woodland products. Coppicing is a complex business, and requires much work at each felling. There is some tension between these possible uses. Animal pasture and coppicing tended to be in conflict, as animals (both domestic and wild) would eat the shoots of coppice. Some type of protection was necessary, thus restricting the common use privileges for wood and pasture enjoyed by the local populace.

This region was probably typical of the general wooded pattern throughout England, except that here stretched some extensive central areas of heavily timbered dense woodland – mainly standards above underwood of a varying nature – along with similar but smaller extents running northward into Herefordshire. The main exceptions were the central blocks (the Forest of *Dene* of post-Conquest times, probably including much of the later named Highmeadow and Lea Bailey Woods and others around Huntley, Newent, Ross-on-Wye, and Dymock). Unbroken woodland covered land where the terrain was rocky or otherwise unploughable – typically that sloping westwards from the plateau edges down to *Wæge*.

Rackham (1986, p. 84) asserts that 'the Anglo-Saxon way of life show woods having a place in the landscape and in human affairs not very different from that which they were to hold in the Middle Ages'. Furthermore, that 'the Anglo-Saxons in 600 years probably increased the area of farmland, managed the woodland more intensively, and made many minor alterations. But they did not radically reorganise the wooded landscape'. 'Intensively' may simply be meant to imply chiefly coppicing, and protecting coppices from wild and domestic animals. Encouragement was given to the self-renewing power of trees by natural seedfall germination, root-suckering, and stump coppice shoots. The heavily timbered not too dense central parts of the region's sylvan cover remained stable, for various reasons: they were valued for hunting, in effect to provision the king's larders with deer and

Fig. 9: June: Woodland work: cutting and converting timber, and removal by two yoked oxen and cart. (Re-drawn sketch from Cotton MS A.VI. Calendar in The British Library, *c.* 1020.)

wild boar; much of the terrain was unsuitable and highly difficult for arable cultivation. Land was designated for hunting in late Anglo-Saxon England, with areas of woodland set aside for this purpose and with enclosures for the retention and capture of deer. The regeneration of woodland may itself have been effected by the setting aside of land (Hooke, 1998, pp. 19–32). [Such areas frequently influenced the location of the post-Conquest forests.]

Anglo-Saxons benefited greatly from woodlands: wood was the fuel of the times; timber was the principal building material, and the choice for almost every sort of household improvement and repair. Among domestic utensils, wooden platters were preferred to earthenware plates; beverages were drunk from wood cups turned on a foot-pedalled pole-lathe. Many tools were of wood. Firewood was readily available for heating, baking and brewing. Tree leaves and bracken provided winter bedding for cattle, sheep, pigs and goats. Coppice trees provided posts, stakes and rails for farmland fencing and the like, and growth was renewed from carefully cut stools (*infra*) – always a renewable resource. Above all, subject to the king's will, the larger trees supplied timber for the increasing number of dwellings, bridges, and fortresses being built or undertaken throughout the country; as well as ships, not least for Æthelred II.*

A very important component of woodlands was *lēah*, 'wood-pasture' – extensive open woodland in contrast to dense woodland. The term *lēah* is from the same root as Old High German *loh*, 'grove; bush-grown clearing, undergrowth'. This Old English term implied in Anglo-Saxon times open woodland, often appearing in literature relating to the edges of densely wooded districts – the

---

* The fleet was active from the times of the kings of Wessex through the reigns of Alfred the Great and Athelstan I to its high point during the reign of Edgar (Hill, 1981, p. 92). Locally, small boats and ships were using the 'pills' alongside (west) *Sæfern*. In AD 1008, Æthelred ordered that 'the building of ships should go on apace throughout the whole of England in the proportion of one *scego* [probably a 64-oared ship] from every 310 hides, and a helmet and corselet from every 8 hides'. The ships were completed by the following year (Ashdown, 1930, pp. 15, 53, 98, 99).

type of woodland which was of most use as wood-pasture, and helped to maintain its character of woodland interspersed with open glades, pastures, and scattered trees (Hooke, 1998, pp. 145–9). Much was partly bracken-covered. Open woodland therefore was a valuable asset and had a direct economic usage in pastoral agriculture. The term *lēah* is reflected in many place-names ending in '-ley' (Gelling, 1992) – local examples being Huntley, Beachley, Flaxley, and Rodley.*

A number of other Old English words for woodland, many of them with precise meanings (and later responsible for some local place-names) include: *wald* and *wudu* probably indicating extensive woodlands, while woods of smaller dimensions had terms (used in the region) such as *graf*, 'a grove, a copse'; *bearse*, 'woodland enclosure' (local example The Bearse Wood); *holt*, 'a wood, a thicket' (Buckholt); *hyrst*, 'a wooded hillock' or 'an upland wood' (Beechenhurst); *hangra*, 'a wood on a steep hillside' (Hangerberry), and *fyrhth*. The meaning of some of the various forms is not precisely known (Gelling, 1984).

The woods of open character would have been of much greater use to Anglo-Saxon peasants than dense woods. In them, deer and domestic stock could graze the open pastures between the trees. The apparent conflict between tree and animal meant that a balance had to be achieved in the case of wood-pasture. Rackham (1986, p. 120) notes that 'the more trees there are, the less abundant and the worse will be the pasture; and the more animals there are, the less likely saplings [natural regeneration] or coppice shoots are to survive to produce a new generation of trees'. Because of this, woods used as wood-pasture generated different kinds of trees and other plants to those that were not pastured. Trees show a distinct browse-line where animals eat leaves and branches that they can reach; the height of line reflects the species of animal

---

* A modern example, unplanned, of *lēah* has more recently developed immediately west of The Speech House.

browsing. Incidentally there may have been instances of pollarding of trees – repeated removal of tops and branches, planning for renewal; but this operation was difficult, and might have been avoided: abundant wood resources were available.

The substantial stretches of woodland comprised almost wholly broadleaved, deciduous trees: sessile oak, ash, birch, wych elm, sallow, lime (pry) especially in the valley course of *Wæge*, alder, hazel, (field) maple, service, and hawthorn; the only evergreen was holly. References to beech and chestnut are less common. Yew (rare) was the only conifer, an evergreen. The woods varied in structure and age: timber trees, coppice-woods, and wood-pastures. There were also scrub-covered ground and thickets with some gorse, broom, heather, bilberry, and bracken; in other words, '. . . woodland in some places dense, in others thinly stocked, the whole being interspersed with scrub, thicket, and patches of ground vegetation' (Hart, *Royal Forest*, p. 236). Not everywhere was there a continuous expanse of large timber-sized trees (incidentally, they could prove difficult when clearing was undertaken for arable cultivation, being difficult to remove with the then small axes and other implements; yet large trees were to prove invaluable in later centuries for increased ship-building, as well as for dwellings, castles, bridges, fortresses, and other necessities). Some of the woods would have been of younger age groups, in particular where coppicing followed by regrowth had been undertaken, or arable land had been abandoned and became naturally regenerated with trees.

The central large block of heavily timbered dense woodland lay unsettled, with hardly any authorized population; and not attached to any neighbouring manor or settlement, because the only benefits within it belonged to the king. [It formed approximately the present-day named English Bicknor, Ruardean, Mitcheldean, Cinderford, Flaxley, Bream, St Briavels, Newland, and Coleford.] On the fringe of those areas lay open woodland with various land-units within or near them – the manors or other settlements having somewhat ill-defined woodland privileges acknowledged by the king. A few land-units were near comparatively small areas of neighbouring woodland enabling their occupiers to benefit from timber and wood for fuel, fencing, and the building and repair of dwellings and farm buildings. The community probably had permission to remove a recognized amount of timber each year, and to pasture in the woods so many domestic animals; together with autumn foraging by their swine (from Norman times, termed 'pannage') [Fig. 14(c)].* However, little record of Anglo-Saxon woodland administration and regulation has been found for this region.

For the appropriate customary use of the products of the woodlands, there would have been some procedure whereby the Anglo-Saxon peasant could obtain, say, an oak for his house-building, and poles and the like for various purposes – probably by permission of the sheriff and by view of one or more officials. Some peasants were probably adept at felling and converting large trees as well as poles and underwood. They knew which were the tough species, *āc* oak, *bēce* beech, and *iw* yew; those which could be easily cleft, *æsc* ash, and *cist* or *cisten* chestnut; those which could be used to tie bundles, *haesel* hazel, and those which likewise had pliable properties, mainly *æsc* ash.

Individual trees scattered around the countryside acted as well-known local boundary landmarks (sometimes in charters, e.g. that of Tidenham in AD 956) – especially the oak, ash, hawthorn, and yew.

Grubbing up of woodland for arable cultivation (later termed assarting)** was frequently undertaken. When the peasants did not want to clear the woodland for agricultural cultivation or for

---

* The value of woodland for foraging by pigs is included in the seventh-century laws of Ine of Wessex (Attenborough, 1922, pp. 50–1) where it is noted that a fine of 60 shillings was to be imposed upon those found cutting down a tree that could shelter 30 pigs. Fines were also imposed on anyone found destroying trees by fire. [Pannage of pigs, under regulations, remains a privilege exercised in the Forest of Dean, the season being 25 September to 22 November.]

** Assarting from 1066 was illegal and punishable. In the west of the region in later years it is typified by that *c.* 1220 whereby Welington was enlarged by Newland (*Nova terra*). Many other typical examples are recorded for *c.* 1244 in Hart, *The New Regard*, No. 15.

grazing of their domestic animals – and were benefiting by a regular supply of timber, poles, and fuel for heating, baking and charcoaling (chiefly to smelt iron-ore) they were anxious when felling any of the trees to ensure that they regrew from the stools. Hence felling was probably when the sap was dormant (October to March). Sufficient protection of the stools was achieved by some means against wild and domestic animals.*

A local trade existed for timber, poles and other woodland products; also a modest export trade: in 1086 on *Wæge* a toll was levied by the king on 'ships going into the woodland' (*DB Glouc.*, f. 162a).

Domesday Survey 1086 gives no description or measurement of the extensive main woodlands; they were simply noted as being in 'the forest', a term not used in England until after the Conquest in 1066.** How much woodland was extant in the region in about the

---

* As to coppicing, Henry III on 8 February 1237 ordered the Constable of St Briavels Castle, Warden of the Forest of Dean, 'to take care that in the season when the underwood should be cut, it should be so cut to grow again (*revenire*) and that no damage should befall the coppice (*coepecia*) – an early silvicultural regulation. Underwood to sustain movable ('itinerant') forges was to be of 'thorns, [field] maple, hazel and other species', no oak, chestnut or ash was to be cut down, 'and the places so assigned shall be well and sufficiently enclosed so that no beasts shall enter to browse them', confirming that the king realized the harm his deer could do to the new growth. (Hart, *Royal Forest*, pp. 29–30; *Cal. Close Rolls*, 54, 1234–7, p. 416.)

** Smaller woodlands, sometimes allocated to manors, were measured by average length and breadth in terms of leagues (one and a half miles) and furlongs (220 yards, an eighth of a mile), but were not otherwise described. The measurements were crude, taking no note of shape or content. Rackham (1986, p. 75) suggests that these measurements can be converted to modern acres on the basis that a Domesday woodland acre was 1.2 modern acres, and the area of an irregular wood is, on average, 0.7 times its length times breadth. Darby and Terrett (eds., 1954, p. 26) point out that 'the exact significance of the entries is far from clear, and we cannot hope to convert them into modern acreages'. They plotted them diagrammatically. The best informed conjecture for this region is, first, that there were substantial areas of woodland attached to Tidenham (*Glouc.*, f. 164a), Huntley (f. 167a), Tibberton (f. 167a) and Dymock (f. 164a); second, there were medium-sized woodlands at Lydney (f. 164a), *Aluredestone* (f. 166d), [Little] Lydney, later St Briavels (f. 167a), Churcham and 'Morton' (f. 165c), Highnam (f. 164c), and Newent (f. 166a). Third, small woodlands were at Newnham (f. 167a), Wyegate (f. 166d) and Woolaston (f. 167a).

year 1000 is a matter for conjecture. Attempts have been made to estimate from Domesday Book 1086 the extent or percentage of woodland and wood-pasture in Gloucestershire, e.g. Darby (1954, pp. 26, 27), Taylor (1887–9), and Grundy (1936, pp. 56–155). Rackham's (1986, p. 78) calculation for Gloucestershire was 14 per cent; Herefordshire about 8 per cent; and Worcestershire about 40 per cent. All commented on the calculation difficulties involved. An informed conjecture for the region – part Gloucestershire, part Herefordshire – is 25 per cent woodland of various structures and conditions.

From an aesthetic viewpoint, the wooded parts of the region according to season had a patchwork cloak of many variable colours and hues. Their almost totally broadleaved trees, all deciduous except the holly, were supplanted by the only conifer – the then rare yew, an evergreen. The generally dull winter scene was somewhat relieved by the greenery and berries of the yews and hollies, ivy, and seed heads of wild clematis, and the bark and twigs of silver and black birches, berries of rowan, and carpets of decaying leaves, grass and bracken. Late winter brought the silver and yellow flowers of the sallow and the yellow catkins of the hazel, followed by the white blossoms of wild cherry (gean), hawthorn and possibly blackthorn, the changing browns and greens of the birch, and the flushes of the oak, ash, beech, sweet chestnut, alder and other broadleaves. In summer, the woods were crowned with a green mantle of tree foliage, enriched by carpets of bluebells and renewed bracken, followed by stretches of foxgloves. Ere summer was forgotten, the glory of autumn fell on the woodlands – a rich mingling of brown, russet-reds and golden yellow, heralding a fall of foliage, acorns, beechmast, chestnuts, other nuts, and fruits (benefiting domestic and wild animals). Ceaselessly the rhythm of the woodland beauty and utility recurred as the seasons waxed and waned. The non-wooded areas – outside the cultivated settlements – would have been partly covered by gorse, broom, heather, bilberry, and much scrub. Elsewhere stretched grassed areas, marshes, and rocky patches.

'WASTE'

'Waste' was the general term often used after the Norman Conquest in 1066 for one-time cultivated land settlements which for some reason had been neglected, discarded and depopulated. The land reverted by natural process to grass, scrub and tree cover; and the Conqueror ordered it to be returned to his woodland within his *forest* (virtually his game preserve). Sometimes the depopulation was the result of deliberate royal policy, or solely the family's decision (including probably that of the absent lord in whose name it had been held). Some land may have been abandoned for other reasons: run-down marginal soils, poor crops, drought, fire, pests, diseases, or damage by deer; or a social split-up of the relevant families, or illness or death. The population appear to have simply moved – to destinations unknown. There are several examples of 'waste' in the region pre-Conquest 1066 and by 1086.*

HUNTING

In Anglo-Saxon times, the woods held many deer and wild boar – potentially renewable resources. Wolves were also around and would

---

* 'Waste' in the region included: (a) Pre-Conquest 1066: the following three adjacent manors 'were waste and are still in the king's woodland (*silua regis*)' – *Brocote* [Lower Redbrook on Wye], 2½ hides, [Upper Redbrook] 1 hide, and Staunton, 1 hide. (*DB Herefds.*, f,. 181b.) Also (f. 182a) the manor of 'Whippington' [north of Staunton], 3 hides 'are waste and were waste'. Obviously the last four manors, respectively of 2½, 1, 1, and 3 hides, in Herefordshire had become waste. The territory of the four manors were later transferred to Gloucestershire (see Hart, *The New Regard*, No. 15). A minor relevant record is that of Walford (noted in *DB Shropshire*, f. 260) which 'was found waste'; but in *DB Herefds.*, f. 182a it is stated that 'In Walford the villagers pay 10s. for the waste land'. (b) There is no direct mention of 'waste' in *DB Glouc.*, but by 1086 Wyegate, 6 hides, 'is, by the king's order, in his *forest*'; it may have been 'waste'. (*DB Glouc.*, f. 166d.) The same applied to Hewelsfield (f. 167a). Today in the region's Forest of Dean, 'waste' simply means State land outside the Statutory Forest not managed as forest; both managed by Forest Enterprise.

have been heard calling in the night.* All the game on his property belonged to Æthelred II in the year 1000. He could despatch his huntsmen at any time; and could give appropriate permissions to his relatives, earls, thegns, and to ecclesiastical houses. All – and certainly their huntsmen – valued the woods as a source of pleasant and rewarding hunting. What the general inhabitants were allowed to partake in is uncertain, but it is believed that customary privileges recognized and permitted by the king ensured to them many benefits and possibly some prosperity; but the privileges were ill-defined and would have excluded anything which might harm the game and their habitat. Poaching by any furtive inhabitants with its attendant risks of severe punishment under 'royal law' is likely to have been exercised: need and temptation were always present.

The chief game of the woods were deer (chiefly red deer and the roe, but no fallow) and the wild boar (*eofor*). Occasionally there may have been unplanned interbreeding of wild boar and domestic pigs. By the year 1000 their taking mainly to provision the king's larder would have been by his huntsmen, who would by command catch, prepare, salt and dispatch (Hart, *Royal Forest*, pp. 36, 37). Birds, notably pigeon, partridge, and waterfowl were available. Animals other than game included fox, badger, beaver, wild cat, and wolves.

Hunting was the principal occupation of the aristocracy (Wickham, 1990, p. 507). It developed into a sport in which the original provision of larders of royal palaces and the like objective was never lost sight of. It demanded riding skills; and was competitive: a man could take a proper pride in his own performance and in that of his dogs, horses, and falcons. The period was a time of heroics – of individual prowess in military skills. There were two methods of hunting. Hunting deer and wild boar

---

* In 1281, Edward I ordered all wolves to be destroyed in certain counties including Gloucestershire and Herefordshire; and coppicing of woods was encouraged to deny woodland cover to wolves and malefactors (Patent Roll 99, m. 20).

with hounds; and flying hawks and falcons at game birds and hares [Fig. 10]. The humbler inhabitants, when they poached, or when given permission, shot game and game birds with bows and arrows, and netted and snared hares. There were certain services connected with hunting (Faith, 1997, p. 94). The king could demand help from the peasantry in making hedges to retain and capture deer, building of temporary lodges, feeding of hounds and horses, and driving game. [Later, in Cnut's reign (1016–35) a heavy fine was imposed on anyone who hunted in territory which had been set apart as his so-termed 'game-preserves' (*Laws of Cnut*, ii, 80, 1); and Edward the Confessor (1042–January 1066) is likely to have continued the constraint, and probably had wardens of some kind (Stenton, 1971, p. 684). The sheriff was involved, and 'royal law' had great influence. Forest law did not appear until 1066, and common law not until the thirteenth century.]

The Anglo-Saxon kings sometimes made use of woodland hedged enclosures to capture deer and wild boar. They were termed *haia* (a Norman term [OE *(Ge)haeg*, latinized as haia 'hedge', a hey, or hedge enclosure], usually three-sided into which deer and wild boar were driven for capture. In Walford (*DB Herefds.*, f. 182a) there were three. In Newent (*Glouc.*, f. 166a) were two such enclosures of which the king had taken possession. The Church of St Peter's of

Fig. 10: October: Hawking, Falconry. Note the two hawks, two waterfowl, and a crane. (Re-drawn sketch from Cotton MS A.VI. Calendar in The British Library, *c.* 1020.)

Between Severn (Sæfern) and Wye (Wæge)

Figs. 11 and 12: Deer and wild boar roamed the region's woodlands during Anglo-Saxon times. They were a valued source of food to provision the larders of the king and his lords.

Gloucester had its hunting in the woodland of Churcham and 'Morton' in three similar enclosures purported from *c.* 1022 and certainly after 1066 (*Glouc.*, f. 165c). Another term, *haga* was used for some kind of adequately strong fence, often around woodland (Hooke, 1998, pp. 154–7). It probably demarcated areas set aside for hunting. The fence probably comprised some kind of pale, or an earthen bank with a wood palisade or dead 'hedge' above, possibly thorn branches laid on top of each other.

The concern for the woods by the king, his earls, and the thegns rarely related wholly to love of the chase (though it was sound training for rider and horse to prove proficient in times of war). More importantly, it was to provision their larders as, when, and where required. Although there is no evidence that Æthelred hunted in person, he probably did, as it was an integral part of the way of life of an early king of England. In any case his prerogative and his prestige were frequently satisfied by his permits to hunt and his gifts and supplies which he requisitioned. The huntsmen, lords, and thegns would have used specially trained hounds as well as hawks and falcons (their eyries protected in trees and cliffs). Greswell (1905, pp. 24–41), provides a somewhat 'colourful' folklore account of methods of ancient hunting. It is evident that at least on the continent there was a ritual element to the hunt during the eighth and ninth centuries and may have continued thereafter. The Carolingian sources are rich in evidence for the royal hunt (Nelson, 1987, pp. 166–72, 177). Hunting was one of the rituals and virtues of royalty. It could offer king and faithful men alike vivid experience of collective action and reward: an apt corollary to and continuation of political and military co-operation. The hunt was an exercise in, and a demonstration of the virtues of collaboration. The aristocracy who hunted with the king shared his favour, his sport, his military training, and his largesse. The hunt's success was celebrated – wine and venison were consumed; meat, skins, and furs were distributed; and a share went to clergy and religious houses. Probably a somewhat similar situation was evident in Anglo-Saxon England.

BETWEEN SEVERN (SÆFERN) AND WYE (WÆGE)

AGRICULTURE

Agriculture was the economic basis of Anglo-Saxon England: most people gained their livelihood, directly or indirectly, from the activity of farming and its products. Society as a whole was essentially agrarian, Anglo-Saxon agriculture developed in a landscape already long-farmed and consequently littered with the cultural and environmental debris of its predecessors (Lapidge, ed., 1999, p. 21). There developed complex estate and tenurial arrangements providing the framework within which the routine of farming was carried out. The main cereals (of increasing quality and yield) were wheat, rye, barley and oats, supplemented by peas and beans. The main cultivation instrument was the plough, improving from wood to iron. The management of domestic animals – cattle, horses, pigs, sheep and goats – was essential to the economy – a source of meat, milk, cheese and butter – and a wide range of materials such as wool, leather, tallow (for lighting), bone and horn; and likewise important for transport and for cultivation of land, and as manure to fertilize it.

Settlements were based on mixed-arable farming in a countryside which had long since been cleared of much of its original woodland. The region contained many potentially fertile areas suitable for ploughing to produce arable crops after trees and other vegetation were removed. Such areas included the wide sweeping stretches of alluvial soils skirting the west bank of *Sæfern* (the Romans had farmed some of them, e.g. in and around Lydney and the Chesters villa at Woolaston), as well as somewhat similar soils lying on a few parts of the stretches east of *Wæge* away from its narrow incised valley (the Romans had farmed the flat plain at Huntsham and possibly at Hadnock). These soils were comparatively easily ploughed and cultivated, as were the extensive flat areas of Old Red Sandstone and of parts of the plateau land. But the region contained much difficult terrain which early potential settlers generally avoided. Difficult heavy clays were generally ignored, but once the plough-beasts had the benefit of adequate ploughs, increased exploitation was possible and undertaken. It is unknown whether on arable land enrichment of fertility was achieved by application of dung, and lime and marl available in the region. The fundamental necessity of finding food for the plough-beasts was partly met by the use of the poorer land on the edge of the arable – wherever there were open woods or marshes they provided pasturage for cattle, sheep, pigs and goats. The peasant farmer was the background to the land.

Ploughing [Fig. 13(a)] was usually by four- or eight-yoked oxen ploughteams. On some sloping ground a series of flat areas were cultivated in modest terraces (Seebohm, 1883, p. 5; Fox, 1955, pp. 180, 218, 219). Examples of them – or of lynchets – are discernible at Madgett and Bigsweir east of *Wæge*, also behind Temple Way in Lydney inland from *Sæfern* (Hart, *Archaeology in Dean*, p. 49, Plate XXIa).

Under the various systems of agriculture, the labour of the peasant sometimes yielded a meagre return to much effort – often a pioneer struggling with barren, or infertile soil. His resources can rarely have carried him far above the level of subsistence. He had few, if any, reserves from which to re-equip himself after a run of bad seasons or disease of livestock, or unfortunate and frustrating

Fig. 13(a) January: Ploughing with a team of four heavy yoked oxen, the ploughboy wielding his goad before and the ploughman steering a simple plough behind, followed by a person scattering seed. (Re-drawn sketch from Cotton MS A. VI Calendar in The British Library, *c.* 1020.)

Between Severn (Sæfern) and Wye (Wæge)

Fig. 13(b) March: Further cultivating, and sowing. Note the mattock, spade, rake, and seed. (Re-drawn sketch from Cotton MS A. VI Calendar in The British Library, *c.* 1020.)

theft including raiding. Probably the lives of peasants were sometimes dominated by the fear of famine. Under those circumstances and the burden of taxation (*supra*) the peasant's position must often have been precarious and profoundly worrying. He might have had a small share in supplying the market for wool – the source of England's wealth – although the Cotswolds (foremost was *Cirenceaster*) in particular had abundant supplies, and was not so very far away. He also had to render 10 per cent of his harvest to the local church as tithe.

Among the varied and rich sources for Anglo-Saxon farming practice are a concentration of documents and illustrations in the period from AD 950 to 1040 dealing with the Anglo-Saxon farm (Hill, 1999). These include, in The British Library, London, two Cotton parchment Manuscripts of *c.* 1020 – calendars illustrating 'the labours of the month': Julius A.VI, and Tiberius B.V. Eight B.V. were used by Hooke, 1998, pp. 135, 163. A few illustrations from the Julius Work Calendar A.VI have been used by Arnold (1967), by Campbell (1991), and all by Lacey and Danziger (1999). In the Julius Work Calendar of *c.* 1020, the monthly agricultural work which dictated the lives of the Anglo-Saxon populace are illustrated and described. In this section of this text are included (Fig. 13a, b, and c; Fig. 14, a, b, c, and d) re-drawn sketches of seven of the A. VI

The Region in the Year 1000

Fig. 13(c) May: Shepherding. Note the crook, sheep with tails not docked, a suckling lamb, and rams. (Re-drawn sketch from Cotton MS A. VI Calendar in The British Library, *c.* 1020.)

illustrations: January represents ploughing; March, further cultivation and sowing; May, shepherding; June, haymaking; August, reaping corn; September foraging by pigs; and December, threshing. However, as regards this region, it is likely that the agricultural illustrations are only a reflection of the farming which took place in the manor of Tidenham, described on pages 4–12.

Whatever the extent, method, and efficiency of the Anglo-Saxon peasant's farming it somehow sustained himself and his family and sometimes produced sufficient surplus food to help sustain the town dwellers of nearby *Gleawanceaster* and *Hereford*; and thereby he gained a profit from his efforts. He generally fed well with a healthy diet; there is evidence of a strong and healthy folk residing in a green and unpolluted countryside, on a simple wholesome diet. Besides his arable produce – cheese, cereals, beans, peas, leeks, and other vegetables – there were pigs, beef, venison (a rarity other than for royalty), wild boar, duck, chicken, various game birds including pigeon, eggs, honey, and fish from pool, stream, or river. As yet, there were no potatoes or tomatoes and no turkeys or rabbits. Depending on season, the diet could be supplemented by apples, plums and cherries, small fruits, berries, nettles, wild grass, herbs, roots, beech nuts and chestnuts. His common beverage was water or the milk of cows and goats supplemented, according to need and

14(a) July: Haymaking. Note the long straight-handled scythes, and sharpening with a whetstone (horestone).

14(b) August: Reaping corn. Note the horn to discourage birds, a calliper, short sickles, and pitchfork.

Fig. 14: Agriculture. (Re-drawn sketches from Cotton MS A.VI Calendar in The British Library, *c.* 1020.)

availability, by beer from barley, mead, and wine. Incidentally, there were no bottles or corks. Wine did not last long. Lacey and Danziger (1999, pp. 9, 10, 26) besides discussing diet, explain average body height, brain capacity, and personal hygiene. The whole played a prominent role in the required hard manual labour.

Peasant clothing of the time comprised simple sack-like tunics with leggings, perhaps having been soaked in natural dye of a desired colour. No buttons – fastening was by clasps and thongs. Under-

The Region in the Year 1000

14(c) September: Domestic swine feeding on autumn tree-fruits. Note the guardian with a hound and horn, and his companion with spear; also the acorns on the oak trees.

14(d) December: Threshing, winnowing. Note the flails, chaff fanned away, recording of the grain yield using a tally stick, and basket for grain removal. Some of the workers are barefooted to keep the floor clean.

Fig. 14: Agriculture. (Re-drawn sketches from Cotton MS A.VI Calendar in The British Library, c. 1020.)

garments were of coarse hand-woven wool – no cotton; and linen was for the wealthy only. Supplementary, when required, were skins of sheep, goats, and other livestock; also, mainly for the affluent, furs.

Wooden barns would have been constructed to store hay and straw, and bins to hold grain, turnips and other roots. Outside the region there may have been a few water-powered corn mills, each grinding wheat (OE *hwæt*), rye and barley (OE *bere*) – grown by several neighbouring settlements.

INDUSTRIES AND TRADES

Most of the region's rural population would have been engaged in agriculture and its associated trades (the two main urban areas, both outside the region, were *Gleawanceaster* and *Hereford*). Other industries and trades included extensive commercial boating and fisheries on *Sæfern* and *Wæge*, mostly small boats plying the waters. On *Sæfern* there was an economic link with the salt industry (salt being necessary for cooking and curing food) – a local process evaporating the salt waters: a salt-pan producing 30 packloads of coastal salt a year was recorded in 1086 as an asset of Awre manor (*DB Glouc.*, f. 163a). In Cleeve [near Ross-on-Wye] (*DB Herefds.*, f. 179d) there was a salt trade with Droitwich, near Worcester, and its natural brine springs. Some such connections are likely to have been evident in the year 1000.

Honey was in great demand being the only sweetener. As examples, in 1086 Alvington rendered 8 sesters (*DB Herefds.*, f. 185d); Howle [in Walford] 18 sesters (*ibid.*, f. 181a); and Cleeve with Wilton 10½ sesters (*ibid.*, f. 179d). A sester was reckoned as 32 oz.

In the ninth century, at nearby *Gleawanceaster* (with its great influence on the region) cloth was being made on two different types of loom; leather objects, mostly shoes, were being manufactured; furniture and utensils were skilfully made of wood; and a potter was working in the town centre (Heighway, 1987, p. 238). The buildings and farm byres there were usually of timber and wattle – unlike the stone buildings of the Romans.

Much trading took place, perhaps including furs, skins, leather, fish and iron-items, both locally and in the established markets of *Gleawanceaster* and *Hereford*; also with Wales across *Wæge*, at selected convenient venues (despite any constraints of Offa's Dyke). There may have been some pedlaring; also itinerant traders. Coinage played an important role in the local economy (see pages 20–1).

Mining of iron-ore (Fig. 15) took place from shallow outcrops (probably at some of the places later named Bream, Collafield, Cullimore, Lambsquay, Noxon, Scowles, Staunton, and Wigpool);

The Region in the Year 1000

Fig. 15: 'Scowles', ancient outcrop workings of iron-ore possibly Roman and Anglo-Saxon, were evident in several parts of the region.

also charcoal burning (after cutting the necessary wood) to supply high intensity fuel with which to smelt the ore and to forge iron. [All were precursors of the early Norman usage: in 1086 Norman *Glowecestre* (*Glouc.*, f. 162a) had to render iron and rods of iron drawn out for making nails for the king's ships – presumably reflecting the proximity of the iron-ore in the region. Likewise (*Herefds.*, f. 185d) 20 blooms of iron were recorded in 1086 from Alvington (an outlier of Herefordshire). The town of *Hereford* required each of six smiths within its jurisdiction to make 120 horseshoes from the king's iron – again presumably reflecting the proximity of the region's iron-ore (*Herefds.*, f. 179a).]

Fisheries

Fishing in lower *Sæfern* and *Wæge* was an important industry throughout Anglo-Saxon times. Fisheries belonging to Tidenham Manor AD 956 have been referred to on pages 6–7. On *Sæfern* were 65 basket weirs (*cytweras*), and on *Wæge* 36 as well as 4 hackle weirs (*hæcweras*). They were used to catch mainly salmon, also herrings, sturgeon and porpoises. The whole created a trap, whereby fish were swept by the tide into the contraptions and left marooned for collection (Figs. 16, 17).

Maintenance of the weirs was a prominent item in the services of the *geburs* (tenants) of the manor: as part of their 'week's work' they had to supply 40 large rods or a fother (? bundle) of small rods, also 'build 8 yokes and 3 ebb tides', which may have involved the construction of wattle-hedges of varying heights to match changes in the tide-level – spring, middle and neap tides. The *geburs* were also required to supply a ball of good net yarn at Martinmas. The lord of the manor took every second fish and every rare fish of value from all its weirs, and when the lord was on the estate no tenant was allowed to sell a fish without giving him first refusal. [In 1066 a total of 56 fisheries belonged to the manor: in *Sæfern* 11 demesne fisheries and 42 held by tenants and, in *Wæge*, one fishery, probably the lord's and 2½ tenant's fisheries

The Region in the Year 1000

Fig. 16: A group of putchers in *Sæfern* near *Dyddanhamme* (after a drawing in F. Seebohm, *The English Village Community*, 1883). Some approximate contraption would have been familiar to the local Anglo-Saxons.

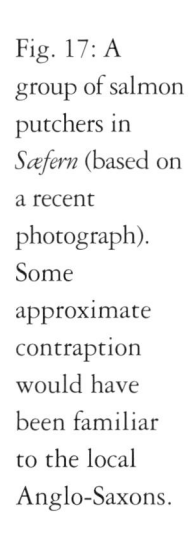

Fig. 17: A group of salmon putchers in *Sæfern* (based on a recent photograph). Some approximate contraption would have been familiar to the local Anglo-Saxons.

(*Glouc.*, f. 164a). The contraptions sometimes hindered river navigation: Edward the Confessor ordained the destruction of certain fisheries that hindered the navigation of some rivers, *Sæfern* among them.]

Seebohm (1883, pp. 152, 153) provides a description of *Sæfern* fisheries as he saw them in 1883:

> Structures . . . built up of rows two or three deep of long tapering baskets arranged between upright stakes at regular distances. These baskets are called *putts* or *butts* or *kypes*, and are made of long rods wattled together by smaller ones, with a wide mouth, and gradually tapering almost to a point at the smaller or butt end. The *putts* are placed in groups of six or nine between each pair of stakes, with their mouths set against the outrunning river; and each group of them between its two stakes is called a *puttcher*. The word *puttcher* can hardly be other than a rapidly pronounced *putts weir*, i.e. a weir made of putts. If the baskets had been called *cyts* instead of *putts*, the group would be a *cytweir*. Thus the thirty *cytweras* at Stroat would represent a breakwater such as may be seen there now, consisting of as many *puttchers*.

This use of what may be called basket weirs is peculiar to the Wye and the Severn (Hooke, 1985, pp. 129–32), and has been adopted to meet the difficulty presented by the unusual volume and rapidity of the tidal current.

Prior to the Conquest in 1066, in Madgett on *Wæge* there were three fisheries (*DB Glouc.*, f. 164b, f. 167d). In Herefordshire, there was a fishery in *Wæge* belonging to 'Whippington' manor (*Herefds.* f. 182a); and a fishery at *Hadenac* (*Herefds.*, f. 184a). In addition by 1086 there were many other fisheries on both *Sæfern* and *Wæge*. In Gloucestershire at Etloe and Bledisloe (*Glouc.*, f. 163a), Purton (*Glouc.*, f. 164a), Woolaston (*Glouc.*, f. 166d), and Wyegate (*Glouc.*, f. 166d). In Herefordshire on *Wæge*: Cleeve with Wilton (*Herefds.*, f. 179d) and Howle (in Walford) (*Herefds.*, f. 181a). In the year 1000 all the foregoing fisheries are likely to have been in use under some ownership.

The Region in the Year 1000

Local Knowledge and the Environment

The region's inhabitants – almost wholly villagers, cottagers, and some slaves – would have possessed a fairly comprehensive knowledge of their surroundings: extensive woodlands, small woods, groves, spinneys, wood-pastures, wastelands, cultivated land, compounds and buildings for domestic animals, the powerful streams, and the mighty *Sæfern* and meandering *Wæge* with their putchers and weirs; also holloways running to and from the two rivers, the occasional spring, pool and pond, and the remains of roads made by folk long departed. They would know the marshes (including those later named Wigpool, Walmore, and Mireystock), and patches of heaths, bilberries, broom, and gorse. Bracken (Saxon *fearn*) was abundant and valued as animal-bedding, and for its rhizomes and early fronds to sustain pigs. Bluebells and foxgloves were present in season. Packs of wolves might have been seen or heard at a distance from time to time; deer were terrified of them.

What was the appearance of the Anglo-Saxon landscape of the region? We can never see the landscape as anyone living at that time would have done (Hooke, 1998). Furthermore, we shall never know if the peasant farmer felt the same joy in observing pleasant surroundings as today, nor what in the countryside would have been beautiful to his eye as he went about his daily life.

Unless the peasant travelled further afield on military service or for some other reason, his abode was the beginning and almost the end of his little world – other than his visits to the nearby market towns of *Gleawanceaster* and *Hereford*. If in the year 1000 he walked up to and around the summit of the centrally-placed great dome-shaped mass later named May Hill (296 m) dominating the skyline [Map V; Fig. 18] between *Noent* in the northeast, [Long] *Hope* and Huntley in the south, Taynton in the east and Lea in the west, his splendid panoramic view on a clear day over much of the whole region would be little different to now. The pattern of woodland would in part be interspersed by mainly farmland. Perhaps could be seen rising columns of smoke from charcoal burning or iron

Between Severn (Sæfern) and Wye (Wæge)

Fig. 18: May Hill – the great dome-shaped mass, central to the region, was a landmark well known to the local Anglo-Saxons.

Fig. 19: The *Sæfern* annual tidal bore phenomenon would have been known to the local Anglo-Saxons. The tidal wave sweeps up twice in 24 hours about the time of the Spring tides, although the most spectacular is during the Spring and Autumn equinoxes.

The Region in the Year 1000

smelting or forging. He would see part of *Gleawanceaster* 5 miles to the east, with the scenic backdrop of the Cotswolds, *Hereford* 10 miles to the north, perhaps Monmouth 10 miles to the west with the backdrop of the Brecon Beacons, and the nearby villages of [Long] *Hope* and *Dene* with its two hamlets to the south. He would espy stretches of the silver-grey *Sæfern* to the east, but *Wæge* to the west would be obscured by undulating terrain. The occasional raven, buzzard, hawk, or falcon may have soared above.

Another probable viewpoint would have been the massive rock (later named Symonds Yat*) above a loop of *Wæge* (Fig. 4) – almost adjacent to the ancient promontory hillfort (Fig. 20). The main view was northwards over part of the region. The Welsh hills lay afar to the west, and the Malvern Hills in the distant north.

Many inhabitants at some time would have reached the mighty *Sæfern* (Fig. 3), known of its fishery contraptions (Figs. 16, 17), and witnessed its annual tidal bore phenomenon (Fig. 19). Also the meandering *Wæge* (Fig. 4), part tidal, running southward usually within its steep gorge, with the fishing weirs therein; likewise its companion earthwork in the east – the imposing Offa's Dyke.

Dwellings were generally of a wooden structure, based on a framework of sturdy beams fixed in the ground and fastened together by wooden pegs. This framework was then covered in rough axe-hewn planks, or served as the bases for a heavy basket-like weaving of willow reeds or hazel branches, mixed with clay, straw, and cow dung. Roofs were thatched with straw, heather, or reeds, while windows were small gaps cut into the walls and covered with wattle shutters (Lacey and Danziger, 1999, p. 43). An open latrine was located outside each dwelling; the 'toilet paper' presumably comprised moss

---

* The first element in the place-name derives from the Anglo-Saxon personal name *Sigemund*; the derivation of *Yat* is from the Old English *Geat*, meaning a gate or opening – perhaps a closely guarded access point, or the gap or groove through which *Wæge* flows below Yat Rock.

and leaves. Lordly dwellings would have been more spacious and comfortable – *vide* the description of the halls in *Beowulf* (Heaney, 1999) also the recent excavations of Anglo-Saxon palaces in England.

The production of charcoal in hearths (flat 'pits') for use as a high intensity fuel would have been a common sight. Likewise the mining of iron-ore from outcrops. There were no known restrictions on or organization of mining – it was obviously recognized by all concerned as indispensable because without supplies of iron-ore (followed by smelting fuelled with charcoal for the making of which there was unlimited wood) there would have been no local iron for the smiths to forge and produce tools, implements, ploughshares, nails, horseshoes, and the like. [Regulations and organization of mining did not appear until the thirteenth century.*] Commonplace would have been smelting in primitive bloomeries, as well as the forging of iron. Scattered heaps of iron-ore slag ('cinders') lay around – the results of incomplete extraction in smelting during previous centuries or even currently – some being resmelted to extract a further proportion of the iron.

Outcrop coal with its heat propensities as an alternative to wood and charcoal was available but as yet of relatively little value; some 'seams' were visible in the banks of watercourses. The Romans had mined some of it at Lydney and elsewhere; but mining of coal, even from outcrops, was usually ignored: abundant wood was available for the taking although more labour intensive than coal. Stone was abundant in many places but generally heavy and bulky for use, yet suitable for many purposes, some being of a nature fit for making grindstones. Limestone and to a lesser extent marl were available if needed to improve the fertility of soils for arable crops. [The inhabitants could not have been aware that below ground throughout the central part of the region lay a huge coalfield (some 90 km^2 in area) comprising many seams of varying thicknesses,

---

* Mining of coal and iron-ore, under regulations, remains a right exercised in the Hundred of St Briavels of the region (Hart, *The Free Miners*).

The Region in the Year 1000

some at great depths; likewise that underground lay an extensive iron-ore field which included long leads, and massive churns and deposits.]

Inhabitants' needs of grazing (commoning) for their livestock and of estovers (i.e. timber for building, and wood for fencing, fuel, etc.) were satisfied without restrictions as long as no harm befell the deer.* Many of the peasants were practical, being skilful with their hands (see also comments under 'Woodlands' *supra*, page 40). They learned by observation and example; parents or other relatives passed on by word of mouth historical and current information – local and countrywide – 'know-how', folklore, stories, poetry and riddles, and 'do's and donts'. They memorized everything they needed to survive and enrich their lives. Very few could read or write. The only 'schooling' was in monasteries but there were none within the region. Incidentally, the only artificial light was from candles crudely made of fats; and spectacles were not in existence. By the year 1000 there existed the first history of England in the English language, *The Anglo-Saxon Chronicle* (Swanton, 1997). The poem called *Beowulf* (Heaney, 1999) was composed in English sometime between the middle of the seventh century and the beginning of the tenth century. A particular fascination of the learned Anglo-Saxon was riddles and poetry (Hooke, 1998, pp. 27–32). A hybrid language had been stirred together by the waves of invaders and a common tongue existing throughout the country; because of remoteness, the region may have been backward in comparison to the general situation. The social circle would have been small. The same Christian names were often passed down traditionally inside families; there were no surnames.

---

* Grazing (commoning) and estovers were probably provided for, as exemplified later (1223) when Henry III ordered that the inhabitants of the region should have 'reasonable estovers of pasture and wood, as in the time of King John before the war between him and the barons' (Hart, *Royal Forest*, p. 37). Additional relevant information is to be found in Hart, *The Commoners* . . .; and Birrell, 1987). [Commoning, under regulations, remains a privilege exercised in the Forest of Dean. Estovers are now discontinued.]

Between Severn (Sæfern) and Wye (Wæge)

The individual inhabitant's spiritual beliefs and concerns – see 'Christianity' (*infra*, page 72) – were known only to himself. The nearest major churches in the year 1000 lay outside the region – in *Gleawanceaster* and *Hereford* – and further afield in Worcester, *Cirecestre* and *Batham*. But within the region there were several ecclesiastical establishments (*infra*, pages 72–6). Their influence on the region is unknown. The apprehensive attitude of the region's inhabitants to the first Christian millennium is discussed on page 76.

The average human life span was 40 years at most. Probably one in three children died before they would have reached their fifth birthday. Food and beverages in many forms were satisfactory. The peasants had their own treatments and remedies for minor ailments, disease, and serious illnesses. The use of herbal remedies was a mainstay of medicine. They knew what plants could be safely eaten or were of practical use – as well as wild hops, blackberries, raspberries, and the like. The lifestyle in general could be reasonably good, pleasant, and rewarding – subject to age, the waxing and waning of seasons, and the weather – sunshine, cold, snow, rain, wind. Subject likewise to the dues to the lord of the manor of free labour and produce, the demands of the king's *geld* and other taxation being bearable, and the Vikings not disturbing the region. There was always the possibility of military service, commanded by the lord or the king. Oaths of allegiance to the king, generally by boys over 12 years, were administered by the sheriff who rode round the countryside as the embodiment of law and order. There were no prisons; 'ordeal by fire' or 'cold water' were practised; a gallows stood near each of the larger towns.

The region's inhabitants in the year 1000 would naturally have given some thought to the coming years. The main foreboding always was the possibility of raids by ravaging Danes. On the other hand, did the relatively remoteness of their region mean to the inhabitants both benefits and disadvantages? To a degree, they may have seen their region as a relatively safe haven isolated from the remainder of England by the lower *Sæfern* and *Wæge*; also with the

The Region in the Year 1000

advantage of dense woodlands. Both rivers could be viewed from lookout vantage-points on reasonably high ground. Did the remoteness give to the populace any tradition of independence and stubbornness – as evinced in later centuries;* was there fear of invasion by the Welsh; and were they hated, or at least tolerated as a mutual trading market? These questions may never be answered. Probably the inhabitants were not unduly concerned with the medium term, and much less with the long-term. [They had no way of knowing that Æthelred would die in 1016; or of what would happen throughout the intervening years; or that the Danish king Cnut would be England's ruler from 1016 to 1035, having married Æthelred's widow Emma of Normandy; or that one of Æthelred's children would become Edward the Confessor, king from 1042 to 6 January 1066. A Norman Conquest of England to follow in 1066 would have been far beyond their imagination.]

Archaeological Remains

The Anglo-Saxon period having followed many millennia which included the Neolithic, Bronze Age, Iron Age and Roman, it was possible in the year 1000 to see in this region many archaeological remains in various condition. A wandering Anglo-Saxon – whether for recreation, interest, necessity, trading, or even poaching – as well as the king's huntsmen and his or the sheriff's officials – are likely to have come across some of the remnants dating from the time of folk long departed (Map V, see page 68).

From early times several large upright megaliths stood within the region: The Broadstone [Fig. 20(b), overleaf] on the west bank of *Sæfern* east of Stroat (Hart, *Archaeology in Dean*, 1967, p. 22, Plate

---

* The effect of the remoteness of the region on its populace, particularly in later centuries, is commented upon in Hart, *The Commoners . . .*, p. xiii.

Between Severn (Sæfern) and Wye (Wæge)

20(a) The Longstone megalith between Staunton and Coleford.

20(b) The Broadstone megalith east of Stroat (*Stræt*) alongside (west of) *Saefern*.

20(c) The Cwm Stone (perhaps a megalith) at Huntsham, close to *Wæge*, at the northern tip of the great meander core of Lower Devonian Sandstone.

Fig. 20: The above vertical stones would have been well known to the local Anglo-Saxons.

The Region in the Year 1000

XIa); the Longstone [Fig. 20a] between Staunton and Coleford (*ibid.*, p. 7, Plate Vc); the Longstone between Bream and St Briavels (until demolished it stood on today's Closeturf Farm) (*ibid.*, pp. 7, 8); and the Craddock Stone east of Clearwell. The Cwm Stone, perhaps a megalith [Fig. 20(c)], stood at Huntsham (*ibid.*, pp. 7, 8, Plate VIa).

Visible too would be the mound of the Middle Bronze Age barrow on Tidenham Chase (*ibid.*, pp. 4, 6, 9, 11, Plate VIIIb); the Iron Age Welshbury Camp near Flaxley (*ibid.*, pp. 16, 17, Fig. 3, Plate VIb); the early Iron Age promontory hillfort [Fig. 21] near Symonds Yat Rock lying across the neck of the peninsula formed by a loop in *Wæge* (*ibid.*, pp. 16, 17, Fig. 2, Plate IXb); the promontory hillfort at Lancaut; and the many hollow-ways, in continuing use, chiefly running to and from *Sæfern* (*ibid.*, pp. 13, 21, 22).

Fig. 21: Part of the remains of the Iron Age promontory hillfort southwest of Symonds Yat Rock would have been well known to the local Anglo-Saxons.

Between Severn (Sæfern) and Wye (Wæge)

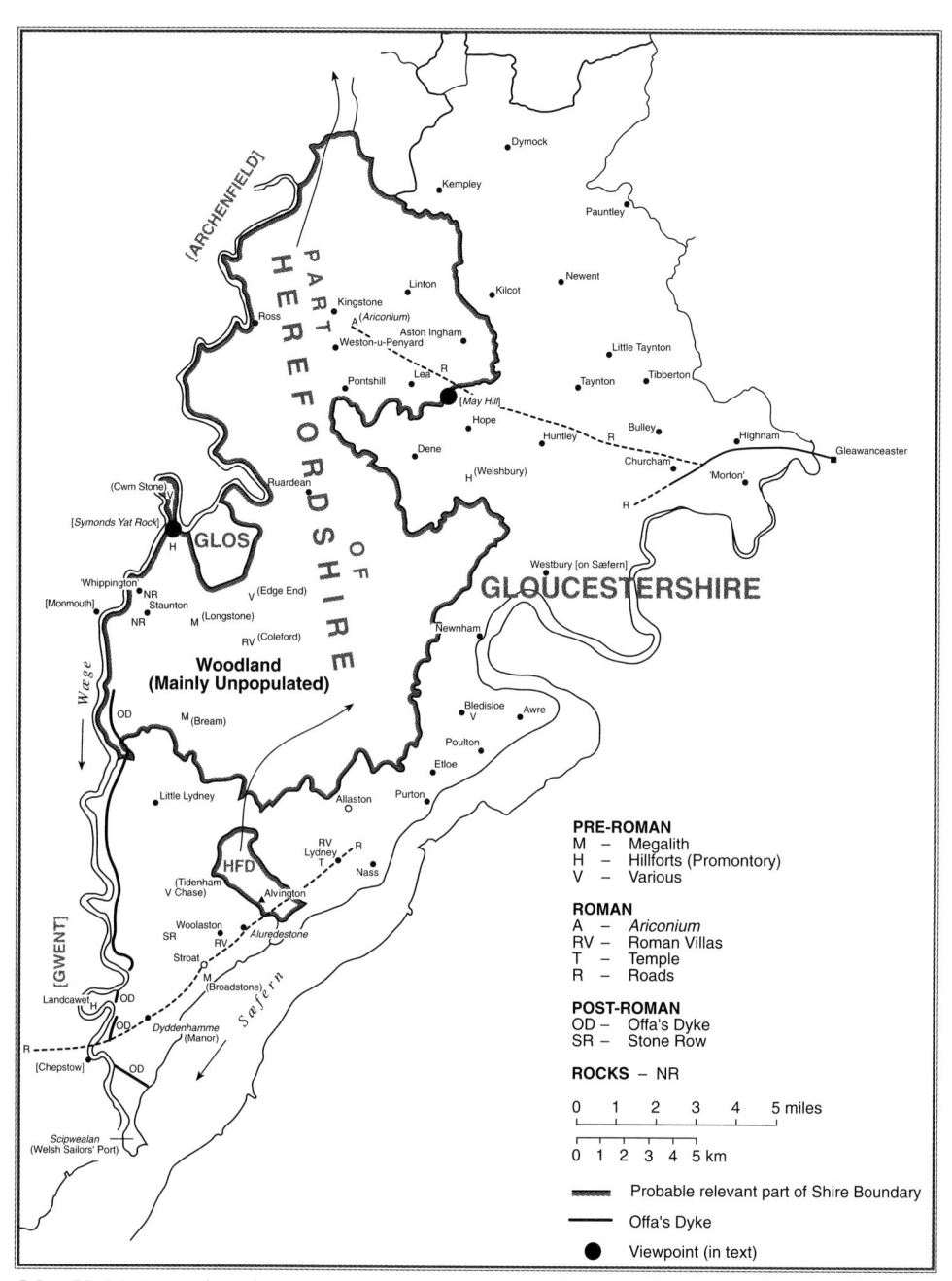

Map V: Major archaeological remains betwixt Anglo-Saxon Lower *Sæfern* and *Wæge* in about the year 1000. Modern spellings when the Anglo-Saxon spelling is not known. Place-names in [ ] brackets are to assist location.

The Region in the Year 1000

Dating from Roman or later times there would be visible: some 'scowles', ancient shallow outcrop workings of iron-ore (*ibid.*, p. 23, Plate XVIIIa); the sprawling remains of Park Farm Roman Villa near Lydney (*ibid.*, p. 25); the Woolaston Chesters Roman Villa (*ibid.*, pp. 25, 28, 43, Fig. 7, Plate XIIc); the Lydney Roman Temple and complex (*ibid.*, pp. 29–32, Figs. 8, 9, 10, Plates XVa, b); the Huntsham Roman Villa (*ibid.*, p. 33); the villa south of Coleford; *Ariconium*, the remains of an extensive Roman iron-smelting town near Weston-under-Penyard (*ibid.*, pp. 23, 41); and Roman roads (*ibid.*, pp. 33–41) particularly that running westwards from *Gleawanceaster* to south Wales crossing a wooden bridge over *Wæge* at *Striguil* (north of modern Chepstow). Visible too would have been some of the remains of the Anglo-Saxon 'Stone Row' west of Stroat (Fig. 4), forming part of the northern boundary of Tidenham manor (*ibid.*, pp. 22, 48, Plate XIb); also the somewhat deteriorating or at least scrub-covered Offa's Dyke running along the left (east) bank of *Wæge* (*ibid.*, pp. 47, 48, Fig. 12).

In the region, possibly existed an occasional Anglo-Saxon fascinated and sometimes puzzled by, and continually on the lookout for, relics left behind from history – coming unexpectedly to light from bits and pieces lost or discarded in the course of 5,000 years or so of human habitation. Perhaps some flints worked by neolithic man, 'the inventor of agriculture'; a Bronze Age small axe-head; a few Roman coins, slightly frayed at the edges by the wear of centuries, but still bearing recognizable images; some perfectly cut cubes of mosaic; or a few terracotta fragments; or Roman objects used as talismans.

Very few Anglo-Saxon artefacts have been found in the region: rusty spearheads,* occasional coins, and small pieces of pottery

---

* Three Anglo-Saxon spearheads have been found in the region: (i) alongside the Dean Road (Brian Johns, *The New Regard*, No. 8, Gloucester Museum ref. A.1109), (ii) at Mork (*ibid.*, No. 13, Dean Heritage Museum ref. SOYDH 1997.26.2), and (iii) on Tidenham Chase (Hart, *Archaeology in Dean*, p. 49 and Plate XXc, Private collection).

(Saville, ed., 1984). Few Anglo-Saxon settlements have been discovered or excavated. Some may lie beneath existing villages and hamlets, or under woodlands.

Objects, not archaeological but well known, would have been the Buckstone [Fig. 22(a)] and several fallen massive rocks lying around Staunton: the Suckstone and Broadstone; also the Near Hearkening Rock, a notable cliff feature (Fig. 22(c)), and several others. Less known would have been 'swallets' or 'swallow holes' – deep holes descending into limestone and leading to underground streams (e.g. in Willscroft Wood; at 'Piccadilly' about a quarter of a mile east of Wynd Cliff; and near 'Parsons Allotment', east of Tidenham Chase).

Fig. 22(a) The Buckstone, west of Staunton. A crag on the escarpment of the Quartz Conglomerate, which here reaches the highest point at $c.$ 915 feet (300 m).

Fig. 22: The above massive rock, and others on page 71, in the neighbourhood of Staunton, as well as the Frog's Mouth Rock, the Broadstone, and the Far Hearkening Rock, would have been well known to the local Anglo-Saxons.

The Region in the Year 1000

Fig. 22(b) The Suckstone, north of Staunton: A fallen block of the Quartz Conglomerate. Estimates of its weight have ranged from 11,000 to 30,000 tonnes. It is said to be the largest fallen block in Britain.

Fig. 22(c) The Near Hearkening Rock, north of Staunton: A notable cliff feature of the Quartz Conglomerate dipping at 40°. It is said that in later years State forestry officials listened here for sounds of poachers seeking to kill deer!

CHRISTIANITY IN THE REGION

The extent and influence of Christianity in Gloucestershire in Anglo-Saxon times is explained by Heighway (1987, pp. 93–144), thereby providing some indication of what the situation might have been in at least a part of this region leading to the year 1000. As a prelude, there was Roman-British paganism of which the only surviving local evidence was the Roman Temple at Lydney (Wheeler, 1932; Hart, *Archaeology in Dean*, 1967, pp. 29, 30, 32, 33).

While Christianity first reached Britain probably in the second century AD, it was not until the fourth and fifth centuries that it became widespread. By AD 500, Wales, Cornwall, and the west Midlands were clearly Christian (Bassett, 1992, pp. 13–40); possibly this region too. Indeed much of lowland Britain was in all likelihood Christian before the arrival of the Anglo-Saxons.

'The British Christianity' has left important traces in the Llandaff records relating to the early churches. The southern part of the region by AD 700 had a church at Tidenham named Istrat Hafran (Davies, 1978; Finberg, 1972, pp. 32, 33). Also a small ecclesiastical establishment at Lancaut west of the later Offa's Dyke, a settlement named after St Cewydd, a Welshman (Wood, Dobson and Hicks, 1936). There is, too, the place-name 'St Briavels' (a Welsh personal name). Nearby, at Hewelsfield, is a circular churchyard which perhaps indicates a Welsh origin (Heighway, 1987, p. 94). At Beachley, in *Sæfern*'s estuary close to the one-time Roman ferry on the west side, is a tiny tidal islet once inhabited by a Welsh hermit called St Techychius (Knight, *Monmouthshire Antiquity*, iii, 1, pp. 29–36). [*VCH Glouc.*, X, pp. 54, 64 refers to St Twrog's chapel.] Churches with later dependent chapels were almost certainly Old English minster churches, e.g. Westbury-on-Severn (chapelries of Abenhall, Mitcheldean, Littledean, Newnham, Bulley, Churcham, Highnam, and Minsterworth) and Lydney (chapelries of Aylburton and Hewelsfield)). Newent may have been a minster church. Other churches were at Ross, Walford and Dymock.

The Region in the Year 1000

Anglo-Saxon control of the western Midlands can be seen as conquest by an elite; and by the mid- to late seventh century they had become Christians. Their most obvious and immediate effect was the establishment of the dioceses of Hereford founded in 676 (Hillaby, 1976) and Worcester, corresponding to the then kingdoms, later sub-kingdoms, of the Magonsætan and of the Hwicce. How far the Anglo-Saxons built upon existing British church organization is unknown (Bassett, 1992, pp. 13–40).

The Church in Gloucester was founded about 679 by Osric, Prince of Mercia 'not long after the Saxon kingdom of Mercia had received the true faith' (Hart, W.H., 1863–87). It was an early Anglo-Saxon double minster, i.e. one occupied by women, alongside one by men (Heighway, 1987, p. 103). The new minster of St Oswald at Gloucester was formed towards the end of the ninth century (Hare, 1992; Bassett, 1997; Heighway and Bryant, 1999). [The Church of Gloucester – St Peter's – was the last monastery to be reformed in the Anglo-Saxon period in Gloucestershire; becoming Benedictine no later than 1022 (Hare, 1992).] When the sees of Worcester and Hereford were created about AD 680 (*VCH Glouc.*, II, p. 48) what later became known as Glowcestersire was divided between them: the western portion beyond *Sæfern* and the river Leadon being in the diocese of Hereford because the dioceses reflect the kingdoms of Magonsaete and Hwicce. How all this affected the region is not fully known. [The area west of *Sæfern* and the Leadon was part of Herefordshire down to *c.* 1020 and continued to comprise the Forest Deanery of Hereford Diocese.]

Within the diocesan structure, there developed minster or mother churches, each with responsibility for a wide area. Some minsters may also owe something to pre-existing British predecessors – but there is no evidence in this region. The bishops of Hereford would have shown a great interest in the affairs of the minster churches of the diocese, and in the eighth and ninth centuries may have been in direct control of many of them (as was the pattern in the diocese of Worcester).

Between Severn (Sæfern) and Wye (Wæge)

In the tenth century there were two major developments. The first is the development of the manorial church. Thegns began to build churches, often immediately adjacent to their hall (or 'manor' as it would be called in post-Conquest English). The process covered the period from about 950 to 1160, and from it emerged the parish system of later medieval England. One would certainly expect some churches of this type to have developed in the region by the year 1000, but no specific examples are known.

No early minsters are documented within the region, but clues can often be gleaned from later evidence. Particular indicators of minsters are (a) large parishes with subordinate chapelries and (b) wealthy parishes. On this basis likely candidates within the region are the very large parishes of Westbury-on-Severn, Lydney, and Newent. Other possible candidates are Ross, Walford, and Dymock.

The second major development is the arrival of reformed Benedictine monasticism in the second half of the tenth century. The immediate impact on much of the region may have been limited, but culturally this was a development of immense importance, not least because so much of what we know about Anglo-Saxon England was written and preserved in Benedictine monasteries (for example, the Tidenham documents came from the monastery at Bath).

Tithe – from the tenth century the render of a tenth part of the annual produce of land – was to the Church in general, in the first instance to the minster churches, and later to the parish churches, not direct to *Glowanceaster*, *Hereford*, and Worcester. Early in the tenth century tithe was explained as taken in actual strips or acres of open-fields 'as they were traversed by the plough' (Seebohm, 1883, pp. 114–16).

Relevant to this region around the year 1000 is the long and detailed role played by Æthelred II and his advisers, as exemplified in the many relevant laws of his reign. In the Old English conception of monarchy the king reigned by the grace of God (Stenton, 1971, p. 545) – and 'in one of his latest codes . . . Æthelred II is made to state categorically that a Christian king is the vicar of Christ among a Christian folk'.

The Region in the Year 1000

By the year 1000 the region had probably been Christian for more than 500 years and was probably more than 'nominally Christian'; how far Christianity was understood is another issue. It is unlikely that anyone would be more than 10–15 miles (at the most) from a minster church. The level of pastoral care is likely to be more than an occasional local or itinerant priest, although the latter is more a feature of conversion periods. Everyone was nominally Christian, but it is unknown how much opportunity they got to attend services. They might instead have visited shrines or churches, especially when there was a family crisis. However, the laws of Æthelred II (AD 1008) urged all people to observe the Sunday festivals and those of the principal saints' days. People were also urged to go frequently to confession, and communion was to be taken at least three times a year. It is likely that Hereford was a greater influence on the region than was Worcester. Gloucester was of less influence, although an important minster in the general area (yet not as significant as Berkeley eastwards across *Sæfern*).

The construction of the Norman Abbey, St Peter's of Gloucester, began in 1089. [Its Lady Chapel was the last part to be built, in *c.* 1470.] In the time of Edward the Confessor (1042–Jan. 1066) St Peter's had its hunting in three hedged enclosures (*haias*) in nearby Churcham and 'Morton' (*DB Glouc.*, f. 165c).

The proceedings of at least the neighbouring large churches *c.* 1020 were probably similar to those recited in the Julius Work Calendar noted herein under 'Agriculture', pages 48–53, and described by Lacey and Danziger (1999). Therein the recitations of saints' festivals comprise a work schedule, month by month, not only laying out life in a daily routine but also dedicated to prayer. Besides Christian principles of various kinds, people identified with the personalities of saints. The Christian festival of Easter is explained (*ibid.*, pp. 53–5).

Relevant historical and archaeological material relating to religion in the region are extremely scarce (Heighway, 1987, pp. 234–5). Only two pieces of archaeological religious sculpture has been found (at Newent). This is disappointing, since the region is likely, as suggested above, to have been Christianized very early. However, absence of evidence does not mean absence of early churches – they were of wood. The attitudes of the region's inhabitants to the first Christian millennium are discussed below.

THE FIRST CHRISTIAN MILLENNIUM IN THE REGION

The end of the first Christian millennium saw no commemorations in the region. In the lead up to the year 1000, reports were rampant of 'a terrifying' comet (Halley's of AD 989) accompanied by fears of its portent. Because of the sparsity of documentary sources it is not fully known how people might have felt in the years AD 999 and 1000 about the shift in the calendar from one millennium to the next. Nor how, if at all, the first Christian millennium was thought about or was simply ignored, or celebrated in some way. There is no certain evidence that Christendom marked it as a specially significant point in time. In any case, only the literate, and then only the numerate, were in a position to concern themselves greatly with what would happen when the year DCCCCLXXXXVIIIJ (999 – the Anglo-Saxons followed the older Roman style of numbering) became a single M. (Lacey and Danziger, 1999, pp. 12–17, 187), helpfully discuss the subject of 'reckoning of time'. The year 999 or 1000 was an anniversary which, by definition, could only mean something to people who dated their history from the birth of Jesus, and even inside Christendom there were varying interpretations of that. Confusion remained as to what day was the true beginning of the Christian year (*ibid.*, pp. 12–17, 187). There may have been some lingering millennium concerns about the year 1033, i.e. one thousand years from the Crucifixion.

The two nearest major churches – *Glowanceaster* and *Hereford* – are not known to have arranged or executed any relevant celebration. The same lack of documentary sources concerns the contemporary situation across *Wæge* in southeast Wales. The Viking invasions were readily identified as one of the signs (or punishments) which preceded the (expected) Day of Judgement; and there might well have been some expectation therefore that the affairs of man would start winding up in the 990s. Focillon (1971, pp. 60, 66), writing of the origin and development of the millennium belief in France, Germany and Italy, records Halley's comet of AD 989 as 'a frightening meteor crossing the sky'; and refers to 'the portents and signs of damnation'; and 'the end of the world'. He adds: 'we find no trace of it in the official documents or in the chroniclers of the time . . . once the terminal year of the millennium has passed, the belief in the end of the world spreads with renewed vigour in the course of the eleventh century . . . the theme of impending doom lost none of its force after 1000'.

The year 1000 may have meant something on the continent, perhaps especially in France, Burgundy and Italy, but not elsewhere, and questionably in England. In all cases, the question seems mainly for the clergy – not for the masses.

Settlements by the Year 1000

Settlements by the Year 1000

To help ascertain the settlements in the region by the year 1000 it is necessary to attempt to discover the manors and other settlements, with main landowners, pre-Norman Conquest 1066. This is now undertaken.

Settlements, with Main Landholders, Pre-Norman Conquest, 1066

Almost the only relevant documentary aid is the pre-Conquest 1066 information in Domesday Book 1086 – that known as the T.R.E. (in the time of King Edward [The Confessor, i.e. before the Conquest of 1066]) information. This is given hereafter, first for *Glowecestscire*, later for *Herefordscire*.

In *Glowecestscire* within Edward the Confessor's reign (1042–Jan. 1066) and in some instances possibly earlier, the relevant information by hundreds in Domesday Book 1086 (translation,* using mostly modern place-names) [the folio numbers refer to *DB Glouc.*] **is**:

> In **Westbury hundred**. In **Westbury** [on-Severn], 30 hides, King Edward had 5 ploughteams in lordship, and 32 villagers and 15 bordars (smallholders) with 28 ploughteams. 1 slave. In King Edward's reign this manor paid one night's revenue [i.e. contribution to the farm of the shire] (f.163a).

---

* After J.S. Moore (ed. and trans.), 1982: *Domesday Book Gloucestershire*, Phillimore, Chichester.

Between Severn (Sæfern) and Wye (Wæge)

Alwin the Sheriff held ½ hide of land and ½ fishery [**Duni**, on-Severn] and gave it to his wife (f. 167b). Alfwold held one manor of 3 hides [**Minsterworth**]. It paid tax. The value was 60s. (f. 168d).

Forne and Wulfheah held [Long] **Hope**, 5 hides, from King Edward; these thegns could go where they would [Free to choose any lord as their patron and protector of their land; not tied to a particular manor]. The value was £8 (f. 167a). Wulfheah held **Stears**, 1 hide, in King Edward's reign. The value was 10s. His predecessor, Wihenoc [Lord of Monmouth], held 2½ virgates (f. 167a). Newnham, 1 hide [possibly in Hyde] (f. 167a).

Morganwy held [English] **Bicknor**, ½ hide, in King Edward's reign. The value was 5s. (f. 167c).

In **Dene** [Later *Dene magna*, *Dene parva*, and Abenhall], 2 hides and 2½ virgates, held in King Edward's reign by three thegns, Godric, Alric and Ernwy. The value was 33s. King Edward assigned these lands exempt from tax in return for guarding the forest (*pro foresta custodis*) (f. 167c). [Later the Forest of *Dene*.]

Tovi held **Bulley**, 4 hides, from King Edward. The value was 60s. (f. 169a).

Tovi held **Ruddle**, 1 hide. The value was 40s. (f. 169a).

Churcham and '**Morton**'. The Church [of St Peter's of Gloucester] had its hunting (*venatione*) here in 3 hedged enclosures in King Edward's reign. The value was 20s. (f. 165c). [Probably connected with Highnam in Longbridge hundred.]

In Bledisloe hundred, King Edward held **Awre**, 5 hides. In King Edward's reign this manor paid half a night's revenue

Settlements by the Year 1000

[i.e. contribution to the farm of the shire]. Outside the manor, **Purton**, **Etloe** and **Bledisloe**, total 7 hides, should be included (f. 163a; f. 164a) [Likewise **Poulton**, 9 hides including Purton *supra* (f. 164a).]

Earl Harold held **Nass**, 5 hides. In King Edward's reign it was not in the revenue (f. 164a).

Siward [the Danish earl of Northumbria, d. 1055] and Winstan held 1 hide and ½ virgate [**Allaston**]. The value was 15s. (f. 167c).

Palli held ½ hide in Ruddle (f. 169a).

In Tidenham hundred.* The Abbot of Bath held the manor of **Tidenham**, 30 hides, 10 in lordship. There were 38 villagers (*villani*) who had 38 ploughteams; 10 bordars (smallholders). In *Sæfern* 11 fisheries in lordship and 42 villagers' fisheries. In *Wæge* 1 fishery and 2½ villagers' fisheries. There are 12 more bordars. This manor did not pay dues in King Edward's reign except for the monks' supplies. Archbishop Stigand [of Elmham in East Anglia, later of Canterbury] was holding it (f. 164a).

Archbishop Stigand held 1½ virgates [possibly at **Stroat**]. The value was 10s. (f. 166d). Archbishop Stigand held ½ hide [possibly at **Stroat**]. The value was 20s. (f. 167d).

In Lydney hundred: Bondi [probably Bondi the Constable] held *Aluredestone* [see Hart, *The New Regard*, No. 5], 3 hides, in King Edward's reign. The value was 20s. (f. 166d).

---

* Tidenham hundred is not found recorded after 1086, and apparently was merged with Twyford hundred by the mid-thirteenth century.

BETWEEN SEVERN (SÆFERN) AND WYE (WÆGE)

There also Wulfnoth [the thegn of Wessex] held 2 hides. The value was 10s. (f. 166d).

Alston [the great thegn of Boscombe] held **Wyegate*** in King Edward's reign. There were 6 hides; they paid tax. The value was 60s. (f. 166d).

Alfhere held [Little] **Lydney** [Later St Briavels], 6 hides, in King Edward's reign. The value was £4 (f. 167a). Wulfheah held **Hewelsfield**, 3 hides, in King Edward's reign. The value was 30s. (f. 167a).

In Twyford hundred:** Brictric held 3 hides in **Madgett**;*** they paid tax (f. 164b).

Brictric held **Madgett**, ½ hide with 1 fishery in *Wæge*. The value was 20s. (f. 167d).

Brictric son of Algar held **Woolaston**, 2 hides. The value was 20s. (f. 166d).

In Longbridge hundred: **Highnam**, 7 hides. [Land of the Church of St Peter's of Gloucester.] The value was 40s. (f. 165c). [Probably connected with Churcham and 'Morton' in Westbury hundred.]

In Botloe hundred: King Edward held **Dymock**, 20 hides. In King Edward's reign the Sheriff paid what he wished from this manor (f. 164a).

---

* The name Wyegate (a gateway to the Wye) survives in Wyegate Green and Wyegate Hill both north of the Mork-Stowe road.

** Twyford hundred was obsolete by 1086, forming part of the Earl Marshal's Marchership of *Striguil*, later Chepstow, see Ormerod, 1861, p. 90. The name Twyford survives in a corrupt form as Wyvern Pond in Woolaston. The two Twyford brooks were later called the Piccadilly and Black Brooks, lying on the west of the main Lydney–Chepstow road.

*** The name Madgett survives in Madgett's Farm on flat plateau land.

Settlements by the Year 1000

King Edward held **Newent**. 6 hides did not pay tax. The value of the whole manor in his reign was £4 (f. 166a; f. 163a).

Wulfhelm held **Tibberton**, 5 hides, from King Edward and could go where he would [*supra*] (f. 167a). The value was £6.10s. Alwin [the Sheriff] held **Huntley**, 2 hides, from Archbishop Aldred and could go where he would [*supra*]. The value was 40s. (f. 167a).

Alwin [the Sheriff] held **Taynton**, 6 hides. The value was £6 (f. 167b).

Wulfgar held [Little] **Taynton** from King Edward. The value was 20s. (f. 167c).

In *Herefordscire* within Edward the Confessor's reign (1042–Jan. 1066) and in some instances possibly earlier, the relevant information by hundreds in Domesday Book 1086 (translation,* using mostly modern place-names) [the folio numbers refer to *DB Herefds.*] **is**:

In **Bromsash hundred**: In King Edward's time **Niware** ['New House' listed in *DB Herefds.* though situated in Gloucestershire],** 2½ hides, came to hundred meetings in Herefordshire and did service there (f. 181b).

In **Brocote** [Lower Redbrook on Wye], 2½ hides, Aelfric, Alfward and Brictsi held them as two manors. They were waste and are still in the king's woodland (*silua regis*) (f. 181b).

* After F. and C. Thorn (eds. from a draft trans. by V. Sankaran), 1983: *Domesday Book Herefordshire*, Phillimore, Chichester.

** *Niware* ('New House') has puzzled historians studying *Domesday Book*. For new information see Hart, *The New Regard*, No. 15.

Between Severn (Sæfern) and Wye (Wæge)

There also Brictric held a manor of 1 hide [Upper Redbrook] and Earl Godwin [of Wessex, d. 1053] held **Staunton**, a manor of 1 hide. They were waste and are still in the king's woodland (*silua regis*) (f. 181b).

Ansgot held **Lea**, 1 hide, in King Edward's reign. He could go where he would [*supra*]. The value was 10s. (f. 182d).

Leofric [earl of Mercia] and Edwulf held **Hope** [Mansell] as two manors, 4 hides. Value in King Edward's reign, 40s. A third part of this manor lay in [the lands of] the Church of St Peter's of Gloucester in King Edward's reign (f. 185c). Hadwic held **Ruardean**, 4 hides. The value was 30s. (f. 185c).

King Edward held **Linton**, 5 hides (f. 179c). Leofstan held in Linton, one virgate of land. The value was 3s. (f. 185c).

Earl Harold held **Cleeve** with **Wilton**, 14½ hides [near Ross-on-Wye] (f. 179d).

Brictric held **Alvington** [an outlying settlement in Gloucestershire], 6 hides, in King Edward's reign. The value was 20s. (f. 185d).

King Edward held **Aston** [Ingham], 2 hides. The value was 50s. (f. 186b).

Gunnar [Walter, *balistarius*] held **Pontshill**, 1 hide; he could go where he would [*supra*]. The value was 6s. (f. 186c). Gunnar also held **Weston** [under-Penyard], 2 hides. The value was 4s. (f. 186c).

Taldus held **Howle** [Hill near Walford] in King Edward's reign (f. 181a).

SETTLEMENTS BY THE YEAR 1000

In '**Whippington**',* [northwest of Staunton] 3 hides which rightly belong to the Bishopric [of Hereford]. They were waste and are waste. A fishery there (f. 182a).

[No pre-1066 (T.R.E.) information was given for Walford, 7 hides (f. 182a); Ross (on-Wye), 7 hides (f. 182a); Kingstone, 2 hides (f. 163a; f. 182d); and Alton (f. 184d).

SETTLEMENTS BY THE YEAR 1000

From the foregoing Pre-Norman Conquest 1066 information, applicable mainly to Edward the Confessor's reign (1042–January 1066), it is appropriate to reason back in time to the year 1000 and supported by part informed conjecture try to discover the settlements in the relevant hundreds or, if not yet established, that earlier relative administered territory.

Landholders in the year 1000, besides Æthelred II and his large family, were his earls and thegns. From their holdings they received services and other benefits. There were also nearby ecclesiastical landholders in the region: perhaps from *c.* 1022 the Church of St Peter's of Gloucester (holding Churcham, 'Morton' and Highnam), the Church of Hereford (Ross, Howle, and 'Whippington'), and the Abbey of Bath (the manor of Tidenham along with its five dependencies). The names of the other landholders and their settlements in the year 1000 are impossible to fully ascertain. Sources are regrettably sparse. Although the landholders in the reign of Edward the Confessor have been noted (*supra*, pages 81–7), it is unknown which, if any, were in being in the year 1000, or who were the antecessors or ancestors of the

---

* 'Whippington' (a brook perpetuates the name) has puzzled historians studying *Domesday Book*. For new information see Hart, *The New Regard*, No. 15. Later it returned mainly to woodland. It is possible that this manor of 3 hides is partly represented by some of the ploughable areas of the now named Highmeadow Woods, probably around Braceland.

holdings. This lack of sources and other relevant information has been experienced by such experts as von Feilitzen (1937) and Clarke (1994). (An attempt was made by E.A. Freeman, *The History of the Norman Conquest*, 1867–91, Vol. II, Appendix, note G, but as he fully realized the evidence is far too fragmented for any continuous account.)

The authorities for the reign of Cnut are so meagre that any list of his earls and other landholders is bound to be incomplete (Stenton, *op. cit.*, pp. 415, 416); and as to Edward the Confessor (1042–January 1066), apart from a few undistinguished thegns and one or two aged bishops there can have been no one at Edward's earliest court who had ever been in attendance on Æthelred II. Von Feilitzen (1937) recorded the names of all the persons mentioned in Domesday Book and the subsidiary surveys as holding land in the time of King Edward the Confessor (i.e. pre-1066, termed the T.R.E. information) and contributed towards the elucidation and the etymological and phonological problems raised by those names; but he pointed out the many problems of the personal nomenclature, and emphasized the need for further research.

Cnut's victory over England (he reigned Nov. 1016–12 Nov. 1035) was not marked by any general expropriation of English landholders (Stenton, *op. cit,* p. 413). But his warriors expected a reward in land for their service in war. Some estates passed from English into Danish hands; and there seems to have been a considerable settlement of Danish noblemen. Domesday Book shows that by 1066 there were landholders bearing Scandinavian names in most parts of England and it is probable that many of them had inherited their estates from ancestors who had been in the service of Cnut or his sons. One of Edward the Confessor's chief household officers, named Ansger, whose lands extended into at least seven counties, was a grandson of Cnut's follower, Tovi the Proud (?or Staller) who held land in this region. However, it is impossible to reconstruct the detailed history of the earldoms and landholders which at one time or another existed in England between the accession of Cnut (1016) and the Norman Conquest.

Settlements by the Year 1000

The vast majority of the landholders whose names are recorded in Domesday book belong to the higher classes of the community, to what might be termed the landed gentry of the period: the names employed by them in the region include such as Bondi, Tovi, and Brictric. The humble people – the villagers, cottagers, smallholders, and serfs – who represented the majority of the rural population, are never mentioned by name. We know very little about the habits of name-formation prevalent among the lower classes on the eve of the Conquest (von Feilitzen, *op. cit.*, pp. 11–33). In summary, of the vast majority of landholders of Domesday, pre-Conquest, and the year 1000, only a relatively few can be identified. Of the settlements themselves, although their hidage is known, it is not always evident whether they were manors, hamlets, villages, or merely farmsteads.

In Gloucestershire: Settlements by the Year 1000 (part informed conjecture):

In Westbury hundred, or, if not yet established as such, that earlier relative administered territory:

Westbury [on-Severn]
[Long] Hope
Dene [later named *Dene magna*, *Dene parva*, and Abenhall]. Subsequently with a Norman castle.
[English] Bicknor
Bulley
Duni, near Minsterworth
Churcham
'Morton'   } [From c. 1022 connected with the St Peter's of Gloucester, probably with Highnam in Longbridge hundred]
Minsterworth
Newnham – an example of an OE *hām*, an early settlement probably because of the relative ease of crossing *Sæfern*.
Hyde
Ruddle   } near Newnham. Overlooking *Sæfern* to the east.
Stears

In Bledisloe hundred, or, if not yet established as such, that earlier relative administered territory:

> Allaston
> Awre
> Bledisloe
> Etloe } All overlooking *Sæfern* to the east.
> Nass
> Poulton
> Purton

In Tidenham hundred, or, if not yet established as such, that earlier relative administered territory:

> Tidenham manor and its hamlets of Stroat, Middleton, Kingston, Bishton, and Lancaut – leased to the Abbot of Bath. Outside (south of) the hundred, lay the point of the peninsula (Beachley) let to Welsh boatmen or sailors.

In Twyford hundred, or, if not yet established as such, that earlier relative administered territory:

> Woolaston, overlooking *Sæfern* to the east.
> Madgett, overlooking *Wæge* to the west.

In Lydney hundred, or, if not yet established as such, that earlier relative administered territory:

> [Little] Lydney. Renamed St Briavels in the twelfth century*

---

* St Briavels hundred was created between 1086 and 1200, probably by 1154, to provide an administrative structure for the area then within the Forest of *Dene*. It is first recorded in 1220 (*The Book of Fees*, i). Thereafter its history and that of the Forest of Dean administration remained closely entwined.

Settlements by the Year 1000

Lydney was settled as *Lideneg* by the ninth century (*VCH Glouc.* V, p. 52), granted by Burgred, King of Mercia 852–74 to his brother-in-law Æthelred I of Wessex (*ibid.*, p. 60) who may have given it to Glastonbury Abbey, Somerset (Finberg, 1959, pp. 1–47).

Wyegate, 6 hides, probably a recent settlement. Overlooking *Wæge* to the west. (By 1086 it became waste and was taken into the king's *forest*.)

Hewelsfield

Aluredestone overlooking *Sæfern* to the east. [See Hart, *The New Regard*, No. 5.]

In Botloe hundred, or, if not yet established as such, that earlier relative administered territory:

Dymock
Newent
Tibberton
Huntley
Taynton
[Little] Taynton

In Longbridge hundred, or, if not yet established as such, that earlier relative administered territory:

Highnam [From *c.* 1022 connected with the Church of St Peter's of Gloucester, probably together with Churcham and 'Morton' in Westbury hundred.]

In Herefordshire: Settlements by the Year 1000 (part informed conjecture):

In Bromsash hundred, or, if not yet established as such, that earlier relative administered territory:

Between Severn (Sæfern) and Wye (Wæge)

Brocote [Lower Redbrook on Wye]. Probably an early settlement increasing to 2½ hides. [By 1086 it became waste and was taken into the king's *forest*, see Hart, *The New Regard*, No. 15.]

[Upper Redbrook]. Probably an early settlement of 1 hide. [By 1086 it became waste and was taken into the king's *forest*, see Hart, *The New Regard*, No. 15.]

Staunton. Probably an early settlement of 1 hide. [By 1086 it became waste and was taken into the king's *forest*, see Hart, *The New Regard*, No. 15.]

Hope [Mansell]

Ruardean. A hilly early settlement of 4 hides.

Linton

Aston [Ingham]

Pontshill

Weston [under-Penyard]. Roman *Ariconium* had existed nearby.

Lea

Alvington. An outlying settlement situated in Lydney hundred in Gloucestershire but belonging to Bromsash hundred in Herefordshire.

'Whippington' [north of Staunton overlooking *Wæge* to the west] – later connected with the Church of Hereford. An early settlement of 3 hides. [By 1086 it became waste and was taken into the king's *forest*. It reverted mainly to woodland. See Hart, *The New Regard*, No. 15.]

Walford (probably 'ford of the Welshmen'). An early settlement near a ford over *Wæge*. By 1086 it became waste.

Howle [Hill] – later probably connected with the Church of Hereford.

Alton [near Ross-on-Wye]

Ross [on-Wye] – later probably connected with the Church of Hereford.

Cleeve with Wilton [near Ross-on-Wye]

Kingstone [near Weston-under-Penyard]

Settlements by the Year 1000

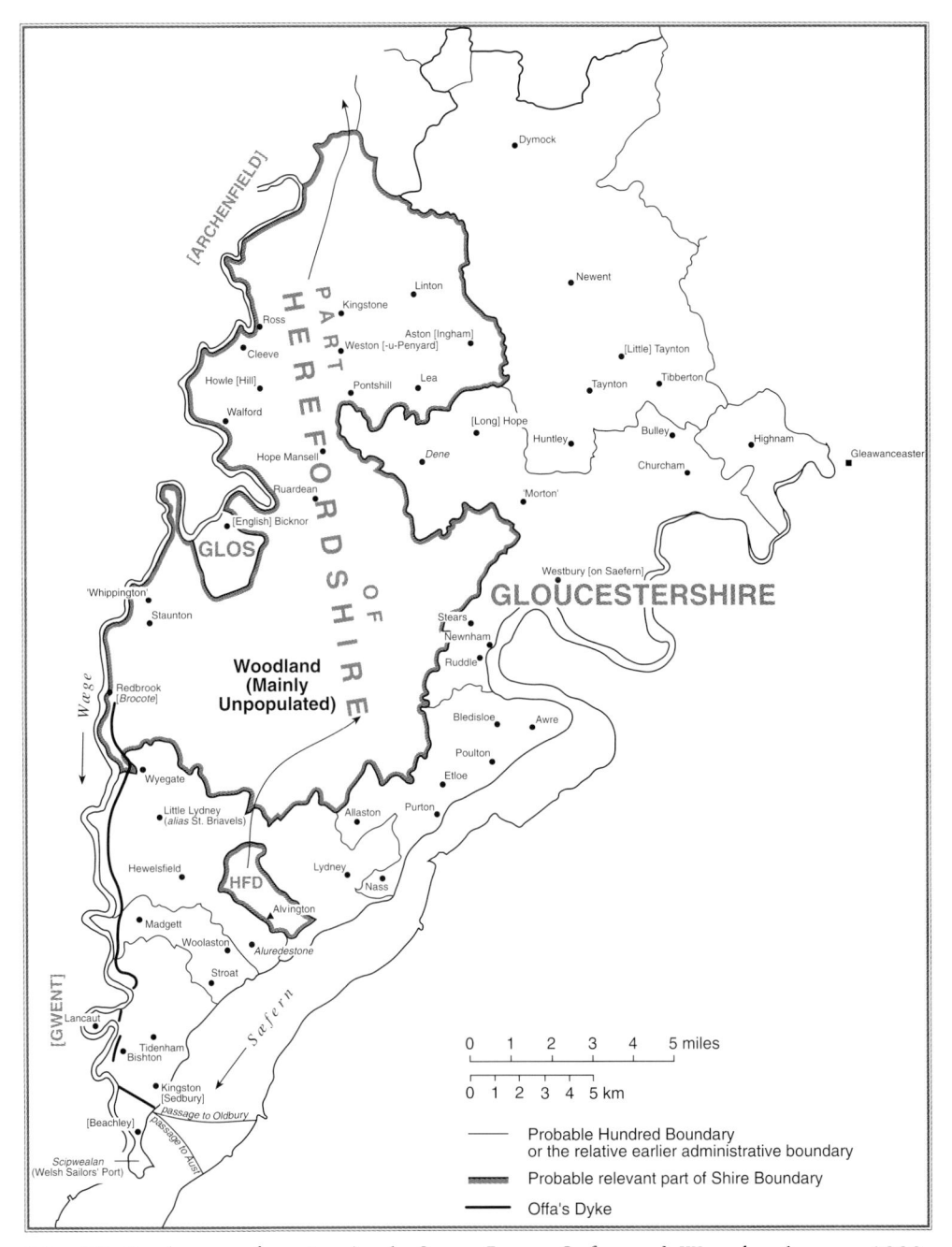

Map VI: Settlements betwixt Anglo-Saxon Lower *Sæfern* and *Wæge* by the year 1000. (Using mainly modern spellings.)

Between Severn (Sæfern) and Wye (Wæge)

Settlements subsequent to the Year 1000 or at least neither recorded by that Year nor mentioned in the Domesday Survey of 1086

[An asterisk* indicates that in the year 1000 the relative terrain was probably part of the main woodland or wood-pasture.]

    Aylburton. An OE name, but the earliest mention is 1176. The ending ton (*tun*) probably indicates an earlier settlement alongside Alvington and Woolaston. The terrain was ideal for arable settlement.

    Bigsweir (possibly Biccel's weir). A household may have resided nearby to attend to the weir on the Wye there.

* Blaisdon.

    Blakeney.

* Bream. Part was an iron-ore mining district.

* Brierley. A small settlement in woodland.

* Broadwell. A small settlement in woodland.

    Brockweir. A household may have resided nearby to attend to the weir on the Wye there.

* Cannop. An ancient ford (later named Cannop's Chapman Bridge) stood over the Newerne stream and was on one of the two chief E/W routes through the main woodlands. (The other route was Monmouth-Mireystock-*Dene*.)

* Cinderford. An ancient ford (later named Daniel's Ford) stood over the Cinderford Brook. Another stood at Ruspidge.

* Clearwell. Part was an iron-ore mining district.

* Coleford. A small Roman encampment had stood in its south; and an ancient ford crossed the confluence of three streams around which Coleford later developed, the first mention of a settlement there being in 1275 (Hart, *Coleford*, p. xxiii).

* Drybrook. A small settlement in woodland.

* Flaxley. A small settlement in woodland. Subsequently with an abbey.

Settlements Subsequent to the Year 1000

  Hadnock, just north of Monmouth. A household may have resided nearby to attend to the fishery on the Wye there.
  Hagloe.
  Huntsham. The ending probably indicates a *hām* It suggests an earlier settlement. A Roman villa had stood there alongside the Wye.
* Lydbrook. Later linked to Cannop-Parkend-Whitecroft (and reaching Lydney) by an ancient track virtually following much of the Newerne stream, the chief N/S route through the main woodlands.
* Mork [an obscure name]. On a stream running westwards to Bigsweir on the Wye.
* Newland (earlier Welinton). Before 1220 created by assarting and named *Nova Terra*.
* [*Niware* ('New House'), noted in 1086 as situated in Gloucestershire but earlier in Herefordshire, is unlikely to have existed in 1000. Later it returned to woodland. [See Hart, *The New Regard*, No. 15.]
* Parkend. Later a park was made there.
* Pillowell (probably 'a spring or streamlet'). A small settlement in woodland.
* Rodley (probably a reedy area or clearing).
* Scowles, The, west of Coleford. Part was a small iron-ore mining district.
* Sling (probably 'a narrow strip'). A small settlement in woodland.
* Soudley (probably 'the south wood or clearing'). A small settlement in woodland.
  St Briavels (a Welsh saint's name). Represented earlier by the name *Lidenege* ([Little] Lydney). Subsequently with a Norman castle.
* Stowe. [A-S, holy place]. At the head of a stream running via Mork to Bigsweir on the Wye. It became a small ecclesiastical settlement. Subsequently with a small Norman 'castle'.
* Welinton. (Before 1220 enlarged by assarting, and renamed *Nova Terra* – Newland). The ending ton (*tūn*) might indicate an earlier settlement.

Between Severn (Sæfern) and Wye (Wæge)

* Whitecroft (a croft is an enclosed field). A small settlement in woodland.
* Yorkley. A small settlement in woodland.

The foreging two lists of settlements (pages 87–93 and 94–6) have attempted as far as documentary and other sources are available to record (i) the region's settlements by AD 1000 and (ii) subsequent known settlements, those neither recorded by AD 1000 nor mentioned in the Domesday Survey 1086. Together they provide some indication of the growth and extent of the areas of arable cultivation in the region, although a few settlements later returned to woodland.

However, it is important to note that Domesday Book does not necessarily refer to specific settlements – it named manors – and, as such, these may be made up of any number of different settlements (each with its own name) although it is likely that the estate name by 1086 was applied to a settlement nucleus. Hence some of the places named above could have pre-dated Domesday Book but simply failed to get into the documentary record.

Æthelred II *in Later Life*

ÆTHELRED II IN LATER LIFE

Æthelred's life to the year 1000 was briefly noted on pages 19–22, including his marriage in about AD 985 to Ælfgifu, along with the names of their sons and daughters. On 5 April 1002, in his early thirties, in Winchester Cathedral he married Emma, sister of Duke II of Normandy, their three children being Edward (later The Confessor) b. about 1002, Godgifu (Goda) b. about 1009, and Ælfred the Athling, b. before 1012 (Lapidge, ed., 1999).

The Vikings continued to trouble Æthelred. On 13 November 1002 (St Brice's Day) he ordered the massacre of all Danes living in England. The Vikings returned in 1006. In 1007 they were bought off England by Æthelred, and ship money was first levied in England. In 1009 the Danes again invaded. On 19 April 1012, Easter Sunday, St Alphege, Archbishop of Canterbury, was martyred by a Danish invading force (on the spot of St Alfege Church in Greenwich). In 1013 the King of the Danes, Sweyn Forkbeard, again invaded England (Lawson, 1993), and Æthelred fled to Normandy. After Sweyn's death in 1014 Æthelred returned on 3 February and reigned until his death two years later.

Æthelred died on 23 April 1016 at the age of 48 and was buried at St Paul's, London. His reign was one of the longest in English history, 37 years (979–1016), but a reign sometimes referred to as of almost unremitting disaster (Campbell, ed., 1991, p. 193). His name Æthelred meant 'noble counsel', but after his death he was called *Unræd* meaning 'no counsel' or 'ill-counselled'; but remembered as 'the Unready'. In his favour it must be said the source of his difficulties lay partly in his father's policies and partly in events in Denmark that would have provoked trouble whoever had been king. His government, even perhaps he himself, proved remarkably fertile in new policies and sensible courses of action. In the end they provided the means by which some of the problems were solved, but not in Æthelred's day. His long reign produced much legislation, some of it pious exhortation to make the English behave better (Hill, ed., 1978, pp. 47–86). He issued at least six legal codes of law, part of which was the basic unit by which land was rated for public burdens and military service. The most famous relates to the jury of 12 senior thegns of the neighbourhood whose job it was to accuse evil-doers of their crimes, arrest them and bring them to trial.

Throughout his reign Æthelred seems never to forget the circumstances under which he became king at the age of about 10. He behaved like a man who is never sure of himself. His ineffectiveness in war, his acts of sporadic violence, and the air of mistrust which overhung his relations with his nobles are signs of a trouble which lies deeper than mere capacity for government. His reputation continues a matter of much debate (Hill, ed., 1978, pp. 227–53). He will be especially remembered as the father of Edward the Confessor. 'Viewed from the year 1000 it was arguable that he had brought England's first millennium to a laudable close. The kingdom was more unified and richer than ever; in AD 1000, in fact, England enjoyed a prosperity and civilisation unmatched in northern Europe' (Lacey and Danziger, 1999, p. 67). Consequently, the claim by some authors that his reign was 'a catalogue of disaster' may be too harsh. A profound appraisal is provided by Keynes (1980).

His successors: Following Æthelred's death his third son, Edmund Ironside (b. 989) became King of England. He reigned until 30 November 1016, in Wessex only from summer 1016. Cnut the Dane (Lawson, 1993) followed to 12 November 1035 (reigning in Mercia and the Danelaw from Summer 1016). He had married the increasingly formidable Emma, Æthelred II's widow. Harold Harefoot followed from late 1035 to 17 March 1040 (reigning contemporaneously with Harthacnut, late 1035 to early

1037). Harthacnut reigned from June 1040 to 8 June 1042 (reigning contemporaneously with Harold Harefoot from late 1035 to early 1037). Thereafter, Edward the Confessor, Æthelred's fourteenth son, reigned from 1042 (crowned 3 April 1043) to 5 January 1066. Harold Godwinson reigned from 6 January 1066 to 14 October 1066, probably followed by uncrowned Edgar the Ætheling from some time that month to before Christmas 1066 (Williams, 1999; Lapidge, ed., 1999). Then occurred the Norman Conquest of 1066.

The Norman Forest of Dene

THE NORMAN FOREST OF *DENE*

The Norman Conquest of 1066. In this year Duke William of Normandy conquered England, and was crowned King on 25 December. He soon granted most of the lands of English nobility to his followers. With the Conquest came the legal term *forest*, also the code of forest law and its necessary administration (*infra,* page 108). The Latin names of the two rivers were *Sauerna* and *Waia*.

The Norman conquerors made little fundamental changes in the underlying fabric of society. The local government system of shire and hundred remained, as well as the system of justice, the rights and obligations of men, the houses, settlements and land (Heighway, 1987, p. 158). The changes occurred at the top: the imposition of a new aristocracy. All the English earls and many thegns were dispossessed or killed, and William rewarded his followers with their estates. Military domination was maintained and symbolized by the network of castles – those in this region being St Briavels and *Dene* (*infra,* page 110); and, outside, *Striguil* (Chepstow). Occasional earth and timber motte-and-baileys were established; local examples were the 'camps' at Lydney, Stowe, and [English] Bicknor.

The Norman Domesday Survey of 1086. *The Anglo-Saxon Chronicle* records that in 1085 'at Gloucester at midwinter . . . the king [William I] had deep speech with his counsellors . . . and sent men all over England to each shire . . . to find out . . . what or how much each landholder held . . . in land and livestock, and what it was worth . . .' The Commissioners' brief was to ask *inter alia*: The name of the place. Who held it before 1066, and now? How many

Between Severn (Sæfern) and Wye (Wæge)

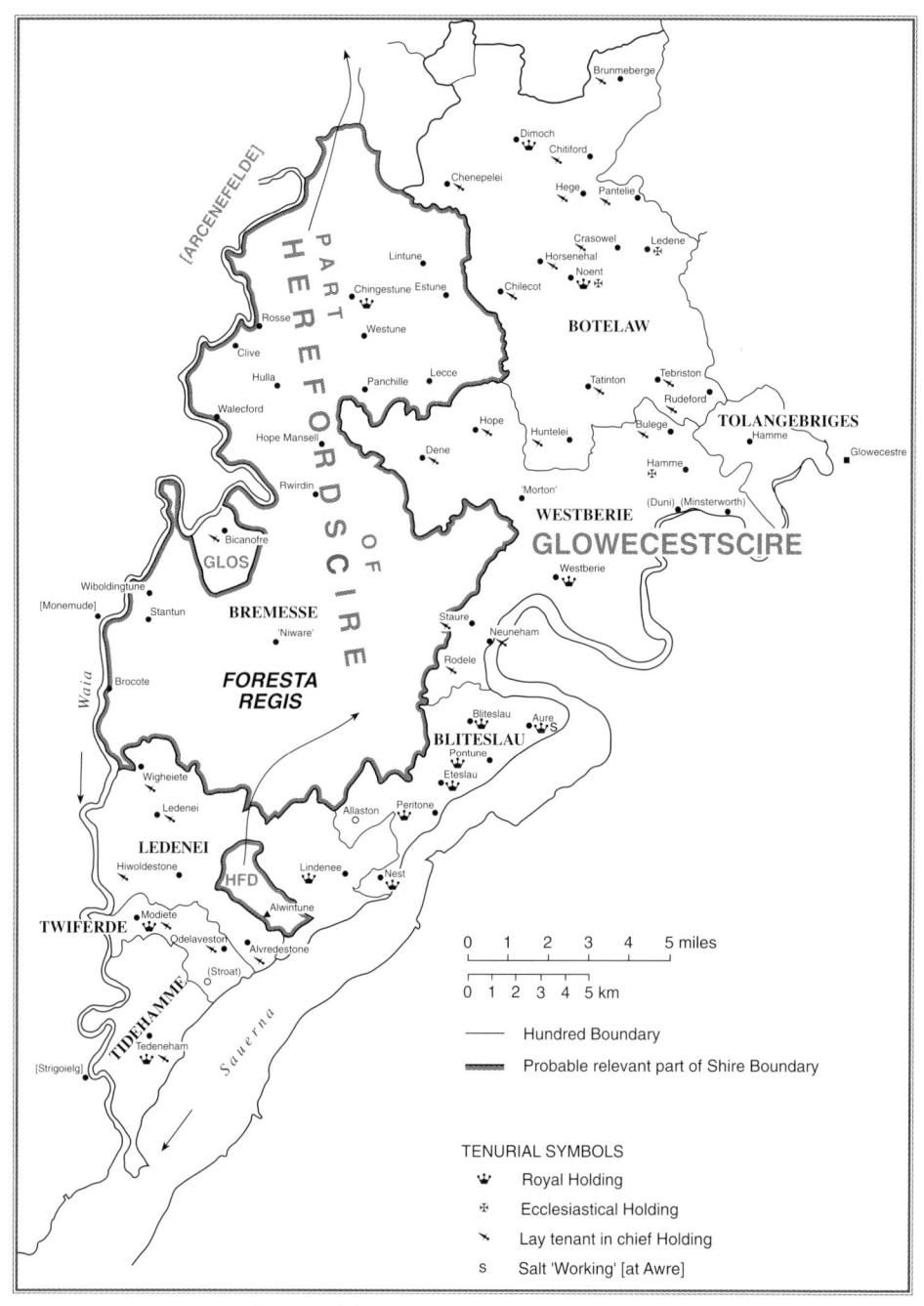

Map VII: Settlements by 1086 betwixt Norman Lower *Sauerna* and *Waia*. (Based on Domesday Book.)

THE NORMAN FOREST OF *DENE*

Map VIII. Settlements by 1086 betwixt Norman Lower Severn and Wye. (Based on Domesday Book with mainly modern spellings.)

hides (120 acres]? How many ploughs, both those in lordship and the peasants'? How many villagers, cottagers, slaves, and freemen? How much woodland, meadow and pasture? How many mills and fisheries? The result was the comprehensive survey of 1086; and because it was the final authorized register of rightful possession 'the natives called it Domesday Book, by analogy from the Day of Judgement'; that was why it was arranged by shires, and by landholders within shires,' numbered consecutively . . . for easy reference' – not least for taxation. Domesday Book describes the pre-1066 holdings of the late Anglo-Saxon monarchs, the earls, the Church, and the thegns – the T.R.E. information used earlier in this text. Foreign lords had taken over, but little else had yet changed. The chief landholders and those who held from them are named, and the rest of the rural population was counted.

Various copies of the texts of Domesday Book have been published. Herein use has been made of the translated text in *Domesday Book Gloucestershire* (ed. and trans. by John S. Moore, 1982, Phillimore, Chichester); and of that in *Domesday Book Herefordshire* (ed. by Frank and Caroline Thorn, from a draft translation prepared by Veronica Sankaran, 1983, Phillimore, Chichester). The region dealt with herein concerns only part of two shires – Gloucester (seven of its hundreds) and Hereford (its hundred of Bromsash).

The Introduction of Norman *forest* and Forest Law. The Anglo-Saxon kings are said to have loved the chase. They possessed so-termed 'game preserves', mainly woodland, including within them hedged enclosures for capturing deer and wild boar. But they did not establish a woodland or hunting jurisdiction with an administrative organization, special laws, and courts (Hart, *Royal Forest*, p. 8). The *forest* system came from the continent and it was the Conqueror who brought it over and established the institution (*ibid.*, p. 8).

The word *forest* is derived from ML *foresta*, from CL *foris*, 'outside', not necessarily wooded, beyond the bounds of manors and other settlements. *Forest* was mostly covered with woods, but also included pasture, moorland, and even agricultural land and settlements (Wickham, 1990; Bond, 1994; Birrell, 1988). It belonged to the Conqueror in the sense that it was created for his hunting (incidentally, to fill his larder as, when, and where required and demanded), that within its limits none save himself and those authorized by him might hunt the 'beasts of the Forest', and it was subjected, throughout its extent, to subsequent very severe forest laws, enacted for the preservation particularly of 'the vert and the venison' – deer and wild boar and the trees and other vegetation which gave them cover and sustenance. Often *forest* is recorded as *in silua*, or *in foresta*, or *in defense regis* (with variants). Supervision of *forest* and punishment of offences within it were provided by a system of officials, notably verderers, and their courts. For an elucidation of the intricacies of forest law and its administration, particularly as it relates to the Forest of *Dene*, see Hart, *Royal Forest*, pp. 7–12, and *The Verderers and Forest Laws of Dean*, pp. 19–21.

As from the Norman Conquest of 1066, the extent of this region's legal *forest* was made to include that part of Gloucestershire comprising the triangular-shaped territory between Gloucester, Chepstow and Ross-on-Wye, as well as part of south Herefordshire (Hart, *The Metes and Bounds . . . of the Forest of Dean*, 1947).* The county boundary between the two shires was much different to what it is today.

Domesday Book 1086 gives no description or measurement of the extensive main woodlands; they were generally noted as 'the forest'; a term not used in England until after the Conquest of 1066. No mention is made of the name 'Forest of *Dene*' but many allusions are made to 'the forest' which undoubtedly represents it. That territory had been guarded for Edward the Confessor by three of his thegns,

---

* In this region the territory termed *forest* from 1066 covered not only the area between Sæfern, Wæge and the Gloucester–Newent–Ross-on-Wye road, but also territory further into Herefordshire, north to around Dymock and perhaps beyond. This extensive area of *forest* was almost joined via the presently-named Malvern Chase to Wyre Forest (*VCH, Worcs.*, II, p. 197; Moore, *op. cit.*, 1982, Notes 3, 4).

the king having assigned their lands of *Dene* exempt from geld (tax) in return for guarding 'the forest' (*DB Glouc.*, f. 167c.).

Naming of the Norman Forest of *Dene* c. 1080. *Dene* (*Denu*, A–S valley) was the name given to the land unit of *Magna Dene*, *Parva Dene*, and Abenhall held under Edward the Confessor by three thegns, as noted above. After the Conquest of 1066, the Conqueror made the woodlands part of his *forest*; and, as they had been guarded by the tenants of *Dene* (and continued so by their successors) the name Forest of *Dene* soon arrived and was first recorded reputedly c. 1080 and certainly by 1086.* In addition, the Normans built a castle in the southern part (*Parva Dene*, Littledean) of *Dene* which came to be known as the 'Castle of Dene'.**

Epilogue. By the end of the Conqueror's long reign in 1087, directive power within England had passed from native into mainly Norman hands (Stenton, 1971, pp. 680–7). With a very few exceptions, every lay lord whose possessions entitled him to political influence was a foreigner. The English church was ruled by men of continental birth and training. The great English landholders and the thegns had disappeared – the victims of a social revolution. The service to the ruler was paramount: no longer could a man of position claim the right to 'go with his land to whatever lord he

---

* Hart, W.H., 1863–87, *Hist. et Cart. Mon. Glouc.* (*Rolls, Ser.*) ii, p. 186. A charter of the Conqueror confirmed to the Church of Peter's, Gloucester. The original charter purportedly c.1080 and certainly by 1086, is suggested to be 'spurious' (? a forgery). The properties said to have been confirmed in it by William I are a mixed bag some of which had been held by St Peter's, Gloucester, before 1066 and some of which the abbey appears to have acquired after 1087 (Hart, H.W., i., p. 65; and noted by Bates, 1998, p. 511). The relevant parts of the charter read: '. . . *et Hammam cum toto bosco suo adjacente juxta Mortone infra metas foretæ meæ de Dena*' [. . . and *Hamm* with all the neighbouring wood which is close to *Mortone* within the boundaries of the king's forest of *Dene*].

** The Norman 'Castle of *Dene*' (now a dry moat with a few trees and a pleasant grassed flat circular central area) together with 8 acres of adjacent woodland were gifted by the present author in 1987 to the Dean Heritage Museum Trust.

would'. However, the Anglo-Saxon shires and hundreds were accepted by the new lords; and the framework of the Old English kingdom survived. The normal operation of what previously might be termed royal law – the work of justice, administration and finance – continued under the direction of officials responsible to the king. Common law appeared in the thirteenth century (Wright, 1928; Hart, *Royal Forest*, pp. 8, 57; Birrell, 1987).

The innovation which touched the peasants most nearly was the formidable forest law imposed on the inhabitants of the districts of *forest* reserved for the Conqueror's hunting and larder replenishment. Within *forest*, forest law largely displaced the normal administration of the sheriff and his subordinates, though sheriffs sometimes did collect for the king fines levied by forest officials; and manorial officials continued their routines.

But in spite of much continuity, sooner or later many aspects of English life were changed. To some Englishmen the Conquest may have seemed a disaster, but not to all (Williams, 1998). There is little evidence of continuing hatred of Normans. Indeed, the evidence of baptismal naming-practices suggests rapid acceptance of Norman rule, though it may have merely expedited something which would have happened any way. Probably, as a class, the peasants had suffered less than those above them. Many individuals must have lost life or livelihood at the hands of the Normans, and some estates may have been exploited, yet it was not in the new lords' interests to disrupt the tenure systems.

There is no way of knowing fully how the inhabitants of this region were affected, but probably the general national pattern was followed. Life for the lowly probably continued in the spheres of agriculture, associated trades, and fishing, but under changed landholders – the new masters of their world.

Glossary, Bibliography and Indexes

Glossary

ACRE unlike the modern acre, could be used to estimate length as well as area. A unit of assessment to geld (land tax); in some areas 120 geld-acres equalled 1 hide.

ASSART as a noun, a clearing of woodland for cultivation. As a verb, to make such a clearing.

BALK the unploughed turf between strips in open-fields.

BORDAR *bordarius* [Norman] a cottager: a peasant of lower economic status than a VILLANUS, villager; normally a tenant of land, 5 acres or less.

CEASTER in A–S place-names, used by the English for Roman towns, from *castra* meaning a camp, a fort, or a walled town.

COTTAGER see [A–S] KOTSETLA.

DANELAW the part of northern and eastern England controlled by the Danes in the 9th, 10th, and 11th centuries.

DANEGELD [OE] a tax on land initially levied to buy off Danish attackers.

DEMESNE (INLAND) land 'in Lordship' where produce is devoted to the LORD rather than his tenants.

FARM (OE *feorm*). Not an agricultural unit, but a render, originally in kind, but later commuted to money or produce, to LORD or KING.

FOREST [Norman] the extent of the *legal* forest changed at the whim of the king (see Hart, *Metes and Bounds of the Forest of Dean . . .*, 1947) either by afforesting or deafforesting. Land circumscribed by defined boundaries and administered by special officials under forest law, set aside for the king's hunting; not necessarily wooded.

Glossary

FREE MAN a non-noble landholder.

FURLONG division of open-field 'a furrow long'; 40 perches; 12 FURLONGS to a LEAGUE.

GAFOL in money and in kind, of tenants.

GEBUR [A–S] a tenant of a YARDLAND, normally of 30 acres with an outfit of two oxen and seed. Equivalent to the Norman VILLAN.

GELD [OE] money, tax assessed on the HIDE.

GENEAT [A–S] a tenant.

GESSETTES-LAND land set out or let to a tenant. And see GAFOL.

HAGA woodland boundary, fencing, hedges, and perhaps woodland enclosed for game. Noted on page 47 of text.

HAIA woodland enclosure for the retention and capture of deer. Noted on page 45 of text.

HĀM [OE] generally an estate, manor or homestead, but in place-names a wide variety of meanings ranging from 'homestead' to 'large estate'.

HAMM [A–S] (a topographical derivation), land partly surrounded by water, or between rivers, water meadow, etc. See text page 23.

HEADLAND strip at head of strips in a furlong on which the plough turns in open-fields.

HIDE the standard unit, generally reckoned after Domesday as 120 acres, of assessment to tax. Notionally the amount of land which would support a household, clearly a variable measure. Four VIRGATES. Noted on page 5 of text.

HLAW a burial mound, giving the ending *-loe*, as in Bledisloe, Hagloe, Etloe, and Botloe. Could be used perhaps for natural small hills resembling tumuli.

HUNDRED [OE] the administrative subdivision of a SHIRE with fiscal, judicial and military functions. The men of the hundred are the members of the hundred-court. The number and size of the

GLOSSARY

hundreds varied greatly from shire to shire, but notionally, and sometimes actually, comprised 100 (or a 'long' hundred of 120) hides. Noted on page 17 of text.

INLAND see DEMESNE.

KOTSETLA (A–S) a cottager. The Norman BORDAR or COTTARIUS.

LĒAH wood, wood-pasture (possibly secondary woodland). Similarly -LEY in place-names, open or cleared woodland, perhaps wood-pasture. Noted on pages 37–8 of text.

LEAGUE 1½ Roman miles of 1000 paces. 12 FURLONGS.

LORD [OE *blaford*] the holder of the homage of his vassals to whom he gave protection and use of land in return for support and services.

LYNCH(ET) acre strip in open-fields formed into a terrace by always turning the sod downwards in ploughing on a hillside.

MANOR, or VILLA in Anglo-Saxon *ham* or *tun*. An estate of a lord or thegn with a village community generally in serfdom upon it.

MINSTER a church served by a community of clergy (not necessarily monastic in character).

OPEN-FIELD *alias* strip system of cultivation divided into acre or half acre strips and furlongs. The shell of a village community which consisted of dependent peasants. Scattering of strips in a holding the result of co-operative ploughing. Usually fixed rotation of crops, with one out of two or three fields lying fallow each year.

ORDEAL [OE *ordal*] the judicial trial, usually of cold water or hot iron. The idea was to appeal to the judgement of God.

PLOUGHTEAM usually of 8 oxen, yoked 4 to a yoke.

SERVI [Norman] slaves.

SHERIFF derived from shire-reeve, the officer who represented the king in the routine administration of a SHIRE; deputy of the Ealdoman or earl; traceable from *c.* AD 1000 onwards.

Glossary

SHIRE an administrative and military sub-division of a kingdom, from *c.* AD 1000 onwards. Noted on pages 15–16 of text.

THEGN lord of a *hām* or *tūn*, generally a villa or manor. A term which altered meaning during the Anglo-Saxon period. By the middle period, thegns were landholders of middle rank. The privileged followers of a LORD.

TITHE, a render of one-tenth of the annual produce from land to the Church.

TŪN [A–S], like HĀM, generally an estate or other settlement. In place-names, a farm or vill; also king's *tūn*, and bishop's *tūn*.

T.R.E. (abbreviation for Latin *Tempore Regis Edwardi*). Indicates the position in the time of King Edward, i.e. before the Conquest in 1066.

VILL word interchangeable with manor, *hām*, or *tūn*.

VILLA Roman estate centre or farm.

VILLAGER *villanus* [Norman], villager, holder of peasant land. Of higher economic status than a BORDAR. Equivalent to the A–S GEBUR.

VIRGATE four to a HIDE. The equivalent of the English YARDLAND.

'WASTE'. Noted on page 43 of text.

WEEK-WORK the distinctive service of the serf (three days a week, but may be unlimited).

YARDLAND the normal holding of a tenant (GEBUR) with 2 oxen in the common ploughteam of 8 oxen. The equivalent of VIRGATE.

BIBLIOGRAPHY

Arnold, R., *A Social History of England*, 1967 (Constable, London).
Ashdown, M., ed., *English and Norse Documents relating to The Reign of Ethelred the Unready*, 1930 (Cambridge).
Aston, M. and Lewis, C., eds., *The Medieval Landscapes of Wessex*, 1994 (Oxford).
Attenborough, F.L., *The Laws of the Earliest English Kings*, 1922 (Cambridge).
Bassett, S.R., 'The administrative landscape of the diocese of Worcester in the tenth century', in *St Oswald of Worcester: Life and Influence*, eds. N. Brooks and C. Cubitt (London, 1996), pp. 147–73.
Bassett, S.R., 'Church and Diocese in the West Midlands: the transition from British to Anglo-Saxon control', in Blair and Sharpe, 1992, pp. 13–40.
Bassett, S.R., 'The origins of the parishes of the Deerhurst area', Deerhurst Lecture, 1997.
Bates, David, *Regesta regum Anglo-Normannorum: the Acta of William I, 1066–87* (1998, Oxford).
Birch, W. de Grey, ed., *Cartularium Saxonicum, 1885–99* (London).
Birrell, Jean, 'Common Rights in the Medieval Forest: Disputes and Conflicts in the Thirteenth Century', in *Past and Present, Agric. Hist. Rev.*, 117, 1987, pp. 22–49.
Birrell, Jean, 'Forest Law and the Peasantry in the Late Thirteenth Century', in *The Thirteenth Century*, II, 1988, pp. 149–63.
Blair, J. and Sharpe, R., eds., *Pastoral Care Before the Parish*, 1992 (Leicester).
Bond, J., 'Forests, Chases, Warrens and Parks in Medieval Wessex', 1994, pp. 115–58 in Aston and Lewis (eds.).
Cam, Helen, M., *The Hundred and the Hundred Rolls*, 1963 (London).
Campbell, James, ed., *The Anglo-Saxons*, 1991 (Penguin Books).
Cannadine, David and Price, Simon (eds.), *Rituals of Royalty* (Cambridge, 1987).
Clarke, P.A. *The English Nobility under Edward the Confessor*, 1994 (Oxford).
Darby, H.C., and Terrett, I.B., eds., *The Domesday Geography of Midland England*, 1954 (Cambridge).

BIBLIOGRAPHY

Davies, Wendy, 1978, 'An Early Welsh Microcosm': studies in the Llandaff Charters (London).

Ellis, A.S., 'On the Landowners of Gloucestershire, named in Domesday Book, *Trans. B. & G.A.S.*, vol. 4, 1879–80, pp. 86–198. [Refers only to 1086]

Erdoes, Richard, *A.D.1000: Living on the Brink of Apocalypse*, 1988 (Harper & Row, San Francisco).

Faith, Rosamond J., 'Tidenham, Gloucestershire, and the history of the manor in England', *Landscape History*, vol. 16 (1994), pp. 39–51.

Faith, Rosamond J., *The English Peasantry and the Growth of Lordship* (Leicester, 1997).

Feilitzen, O. von, *The Pre-Conquest Personal-Names of Domesday Book*, 1937 (Uppsala, Sweden).

Finberg, H.P.R., *Gloucestershire: The Making of the English Landscape*, 1955 (London).

Finberg, H.P.R., *Gloucestershire Studies*, 1957 (Leicester).

Finberg, H.P.R., *The Early Charters of the West Midlands*, 1961 (Leicester)

Fletcher, Richard, *Who's Who in Roman Britain and Anglo-Saxon England*, 1989 (Shepheard-Walwyn, London).

Focillon, Henri, *The Year 1000*, First Harper Torchbooks, 1971 (Evanson, New York).

Fox, Sir Cyril, *Offa's Dyke*, 1955 (Oxford).

Freeman, E.A., *The History of the Norman Conquest*, 6 vols., 1867–79.

Fullbrook-Leggatt, L.E.W.O., 'Saxon Gloucestershire', *Trans. B. & G.A.S.*, vol. 57, 1935, pp. 110–38. [An introduction]

Gelling, Margaret, *Place Names in the Landscape*, 1984 (Dent, London).

Gelling, Margaret, *The West Midlands in the Early Middle Ages*, 1992 (Leicester).

Greswell, W.H.P., *Forests and Deer Parks of . . . Somerset*, 1905.

Grundy, G.B., 'Saxon Charters and Field Names of Gloucestershire', *Trans. B. & G. A.S.* 1936.

Grundy, G.B., 'The Ancient Woodland of Gloucestershire', *Trans. B. & G.A.S.*, vol. 58, 1936.

Hall, D., 'The Origins of open-field Agriculture', pp. 22–38 in Rowley, Trevor, ed., *The Origins of Open-field Agriculture*, 1981 (Croom Helm, London).

Hare, Michael, 'The two Anglo-Saxon minsters of Gloucester', Deerhurst Lecture, 1992.

Hare, Michael, 'Kings Crowns and Festivals: The Origins of Gloucester as a Royal Ceremonial Centre; *Trans. B. & G.A.S.*, vol. 115, 1997.

Harrison, M. and Embleton, G., *Anglo-Saxon Thegn: 449–1066 AD*, 1993 (Osprey).

BIBLIOGRAPHY

Hart, C.E. – See publication titles in the Preface.

Hart, W.H., *Monasticum et Cart. Mon. Glouc.*, Rolls Series, 3 vols., 1863–88.

Heaney, Seamus, *Beowulf*: A New Translation, 1999 (Faber and Faber, London).

Heighway, Carolyn, 'Anglo-Saxon Gloucestershire' in Saville, ed., *Archaeology in Gloucestershire*, 1984 (Cheltenham).

Heighway, Carolyn, *Anglo-Saxon Gloucestershire*, 1987 (Alan Sutton, Stroud).

Heighway, Carolyn and Bryant, R., *The Golden Minster: The Anglo-Saxon Minster and later medieval priory of St. Oswald at Gloucester, Council for British Archaeology Research Report*, 177 (York, 1999).

Hill, David, ed., *Ethelred the Unready: Papers from the Millenary Conference, 1978* (Oxford).

Hill, David, ed., *An Atlas of Anglo-Saxon England*, 1981 (Blackwell, Oxford).

Hill, David, *Landscape History; Eleventh century Labours of the Months in Prose and Pictures*, pp. 29–39, 1999.

Hill, David, 'Offa's Dyke: Pattern and Purpose' (Lecture 1996, Society of Antiquaries).

Hillaby, J.G., 'The Origins of the Diocese of Hereford', pp. 16–52, in *Trans. Woolhope Naturalists' Field Club*, 42, 1976, Pt. I.

Hollister, C.W., *Anglo-Saxon Military Institutions*, 1962 (Oxford).

Hooke, Della, 'Open-field Agriculture – The Evidence from the Pre-Conquest Charters of the West Midlands', pp. 39–63, in Rowley, Trevor, ed. 1981.

Hooke, Della, *The Anglo-Saxon Landscape; The Kingdom of the Hwicce*, 1985 (Manchester).

Hooke, Della, 'Pre-Conquest Woodland: Its Distribution and Usage', in *Agric. Hist. Rev.*, 37, II, 1989, pp. 113–29.

Hooke, Della, *The Landscape of Anglo-Saxon England*, 1998 (London).

Hooke, Della, 'Medieval forests and parks in southern and central England', in *European Woods and Forests: Studies in Cultural History*, ed. C. Watkins, Dept. of Geography, Univ. of Nottingham, 1998, pp. 19–32.

Jones, G.R.J., 'Early Customary Tenures in Wales and Open-field Agriculture', pp. 202–25, in Rowley, Trevor, ed. 1981.

Kemble, J.M., *Codex Diplomaticus Aevi Saconici, 1839–48.*

Keynes, Simon, *The Diplomas of King Æthelred 'The Unready' 978–1016*, 1980 (Cambridge).

Knight, J., *Monmouthshire Antiquity*, iii.

Lacey, Robert and Danziger, Danny, *The Year 1000*, 1999 (Little, Brown and Company, London).

BIBLIOGRAPHY

Lapidge, M., ed., *The Blackwell Encyclopaedia of Anglo-Saxon England*, 1999 (Oxford).

Larson, L.M., *Canute the Great*, 1912.

Lawson, M.K., *Cnut: The Danes in England in the Early Eleventh Century* (1993, Longman).

Moore, John, S., *Domesday Book Gloucestershire*, 1982 (Phillimore, Chichester).

Moore, John, S., 'The Gloucestershire section of Domesday Book: Geographical problems of the text', *Trans. B. & G.A.S.*, vol. 105, 1987, et seq.

Nelson, Janet L., in Cannadine and Price (eds.), *Rituals of Royalty*, 1987 (Cambridge).

New Regard, The; Annual Journal of the Forest of Dean Local History Society.

Ormerod, G., *Strigulensia*, 1861 (London).

Poole, Russell, 'Skaldic Verse and Anglo-Saxon History: Some Aspects of the Period 1009–1016' (*Speculum*, vol. 62, 1987, pp. 265–98).

Price, Denis, *The Normans in Gloucestershire and Bristol* 1983 (Bristol).

Rackham, Oliver, *The History of the Countryside*, 1986 (Dent, London).

Robertson, A.J., ed., *Anglo-Saxon Charters*, 2nd edn, 1956 (Cambridge).

Rowley, Trevor, ed., *The Origins of Open-field Agriculture*, 1981 (Croom Helm, London).

Saville, Alan, ed., *Archaeology in Gloucestershire*, 1984 (Cheltenham).

Sawyer, P.H., *Anglo-Saxon Charters: An annotated List and Bibliography*, 1968 (London).

Sawyer, P.H., *From Roman Britain to Norman England*, 2nd ed., 1998 (Routledge, London).

Seebohm, F., *The English Village Community*, 1883 (London).

Smith, A.H., *The Place-Names of Gloucestershire*, Part III (English Place-Name Society, vol. XL, 1964) (Cambridge).

Stenton, Sir Frank, *Anglo-Saxon England*, 3rd edn., 1971 (Oxford).

Swanton, Michael, *The Anglo-Saxon Church*, trans. and ed., 1997 (London).

Taylor, C.S., *An Analysis of the Domesday Survey of Gloucestershire*, 1887–9.

Thorn, Frank and Caroline, *Domesday Book Herefordshire*, 1983 (Phillimore, Chichester).

Thorpe, B., *The Anglo-Saxon Chronicle*, 1861. [One of many versions]

Victoria History of the Counties of England: Gloucestershire, especially vols. V (1996) covering Bledisloe and St Briavels hundreds and the Forest of Dean, and X (1972) covering Westbury hundred.

Welch, Martin, *The English Heritage Book of Anglo-Saxon England*, 1992 (London).

BIBLIOGRAPHY

Wheeler, R.E.M. and T.V., 'Report on the Prehistoric, Roman and Post-Roman Site in Lydney Park, Gloucestershire', *Rept. of the Res. Cttee of the Soc. of Antiquaries of London*, ix (1932).

Whybra, J., *A Lost English County, Winchcombe*, 1990 (Boydell, Woodbridge).

Wickham, C.J., 'European Forests in the Early Middle Ages: Landscape and Land Clearance', 1990 (in *Settimane di Studio del Centro Italiano di Studi Sull' Alto Medioevo*, vol. 37, 1990, pp. 479–548) (Italy).

Williams, Ann, *The English and the Norman Conquest*, 1998 (Boydell, Woodbridge).

Williams, Ann, *Kingship and Government in Pre-Conquest England* c. 500–1066 (1999).

Wood, J.G., Dobson, D.P., and Hicks, F.W.P., 'The Church and Parish of Lancaut', *Trans. B. & G. A.S.*, vol. 58, 1936, pp. 207–8.

Wright, E.C., *Common Law in the Thirteenth Century English Royal Forests*, 1928 (Philadelphia).

Index of Subjects

The main group-headings are: agriculture; animals, domestic; animals, wild; trades; trees, species; and vegetation.

abbey
  Bath 4, 5, 8, 12, 83, 87, 90
  Glastonbury 91
  Llandaff 72
  St Peter's of Gloucester 73, 76, *and see* churches
abbot 4, 5, 8, 12, 83, *and see* abbey
acres, *see* hide *and* Glossary
agriculture 4, 5, 10, 12, 38, 48–53, 54, 62, 96; Figs 13 and 14
  animals, farm, *see* animals, domestic
  beekeeping 25
  crops
    barley 48, 53
    beans 48
    oats 48
    peas 48
    rye 48
    turnips 53
    wheat 48, 53
  cultivation Fig. 13
  equipment, tools 25, 37
    calliper Fig. 14
    flail Fig. 14
    mattock Fig. 13
    pitchfork Fig. 14
    rake Fig. 13
    scythe Fig. 14
    sickle Fig. 14
    spade Fig. 13
    tally stick Fig. 14
    whetstone Fig. 14
  farm (*feorm*) 23

harvesting Fig. 14
haymaking Fig. 14
manuring, *see* lime *and* marl
ploughing 10, 48, 49; Fig. 13
ploughs 25, 62
poultry 24
reaping 10; Fig. 14
seed 10
shepherding Fig. 13
systems 24, 25, 49
  arable 24, 34, 49, 62, 96
  'open-field' 24
  'strip-cultivation' 24, 25
threshing 53; Fig. 14
Anglo-Saxon *passim*
Anglo-Saxon Chronicle, The 5, 63, 105
animals, domestic 24, 48, 49
  browse-line 38, 39
  cattle 24, 34
  dogs, hounds 44, 45; Fig. 14
  horses 44; Fig. 10
  goats 24, 34
  oxen 36, 49; Figs 9 and 13
  pigs, 10, 24, 59, *and see* mast *and* pannage; Fig. 14
  sheep 24, 34; Fig. 13
  and see lēah and wood-pasture
animals, wild, 'beasts of the forest' 109
  badger 44
  beaver 44
  boar, 20, 34, 37, 43, 44, 45, *and see* mast; Fig. 12
  browse-line 38, 39

Index of Subjects

cat 44
deer, 20, 34, 37, 41, 43, 44, 45, 59, 63, 71; Fig. 11
fox 44
hare 45
rabbit 51
wolf 43, 44, 59
  and see nets, snares, traps, *and* hedged enclosures
archaeological remains 65–71, Map V
armies, *see* warfare
arms, weapons, *see* warfare
artefacts 69
assarts, assarting 40, 95, *and see* Glossary
axes Fig. 9

battles 5, 19, 28
  Dyrham AD 577, 5
  Maldon (Essex) AD 991, 28
beekeeping, *see* agriculture
beverages 37, 51, 52, 64, *and see* mead
birds
  buzzard 61
  crane 45; Fig. 10
  hawk, falcon 44, 45, 61; Fig. 10
  partridge 44
  pigeon 44
  raven 61
  turkey 51
  waterfowl 44; Fig. 10
bishops 73, 87, *and see* abbeys *and* churches
bloomeries, *see* forges
boars, *see* animals, wild, *and* hunting
body height, human, 52
bordar (*bordarius*) [Norman] 31, 81, 83, *and see* Glossary
boundaries 1, 5–8, 16, 17, 69, 109
bridges, wooden 26, 37, *and see* Roman bridge work 17, 22, 30

Bristol Channel 4
Bronze Age 65, 66, 67, 69, Map V
buildings 24, 53, 54, 63
burhs, fortresses 15, 16

candles 63
carpenter 25
carts, 36; Fig. 9
castles and camps, Norman 89, 105
  (English) Bicknor 105
  of *Dene* 89, 105, 110
  Lydney 105
  St Briavels 105, 110
  Stowe 95, 105
  of *Striguil* (Chepstow) 26, 69, 84, 105
chapels, chapelries 72
charcoal burning 56, 59, 62
charters, Anglo-Saxon 5, 7, 8, 12
  boundary landmark trees in, 6
Christianity in England 72–7
  the first Christian millennium 63, 64, 76, 77
  fears 76, 77
  not celebrated 76, 77
Christianity in Wales 72, 76
churches, abbeys 28, 64, 73, 74, 75, 76
  Bath 64
  Berkeley 75
  Cirencester 64
  diocese 13, 15, 73
  dues, tithes 10, 30, 50
  Hereford 64, 76, 87
  Lancaut 72
  St Oswald's, Gloucester 45, 47, 64, 73, 76
  St Peter's, Gloucester 64, 73, 75, 76, 82, 84, 86, 87, 89, 110
  Tidenham 72
  Worcester 64
cinders, 'slag', iron, use of 62

Index of Subjects

clergy, *see* bishops and priests
climate 64
clothing 52, 53
coal, mining of 20, 62, 63
coinage 17, *and see* mints; Fig. 5
common law 45, 111
commoning, grazing 63
communities 10
coppices 35, 36, 37, 41, 44
corn mills, water-mills 27, 53
cottager (*kotsetla* [A–S], *cottarius* [Norman]) 22, 23, 25, 59, *and see* Glossary
courts
  hundred 17
  shire 16
Craddock Stone, 67, Map V
craftsmanship 25, 40, 63
currency, coins, coinage, mint-places 17; Fig. 5
customs 7, 8, 10, 12, 22, 23

Danegeld, *see* taxation *and* Glossary
Danelaw 100, *and see* Glossary
Danes, the 31, 64
Dark Ages 35
Dean Heritage Museum Trust 110
deer, *see* animals, wild, *and* hunting
demesne land (*Inland*), 7, *and see* land tenure *and* Glossary
diocese, *see* churches
Domesday Book 1086, 16, 17, 31, 41, 42, 81–93, 96, 105, 108, Maps VII and VIII
Dunsæte, people of Archenfield 4, 33

earls 22, 47, 87, 105, 111
Easter 75
education 63
environment 59–65, *and see* landscape

estovers 63
eyries, hawks' 47

family size 32
farms, fields, farming, 23, 24, *and see* agriculture *and* Glossary
fences, 25, 47, 63, *and see* woodland (*haga*)
ferries 26, 33, 89
  Newnham-Arlingham 26
  'Old Passage, The' 27, 33, Map III
festivals 75
firewood, fuel 37, 63
fish 8, 12 (porpoises, herrings, sturgeon, salmon) 33, 56
fisheries, fishermen, 7, 12; Figs 16 and 17
  on Severn – *Sæfern* 16, 17, 33, 54, 56–8, 82, 83; Figs 16 and 17
  on Wye – *Wæge* 56, 58, 82, 83, 84, 87
fleet, 22, 30, 37, *and see* ships
folkland 22
folklore 63
food 48, 51, 64
fords 24, 26
forest 43, 105, 108, 109, 111, *and see* forest law *and* Glossary
forest law 45, 105, 108, 109, 111
Forest of *Dene*, Dean, Norman 43, 82, 90, 105–11, *and passim*
  naming of 110
  guarding of 82, 110
  statutory forest 43
Forest of Dean District Council xiii
Forest Deanery 73
Forest Enterprise 43
forests, royal 109, *and see* law administration 105, 108, 109, 111 *and see* Forest of *Dene*, Dean; Malvern; Wyre

127

Index of Subjects

forges (moveable, 'itinerant'), 20, 25, 62
    bloomeries 62
fortress-work, fortifications 16, 17, 22, 30
fortresses 16, 37, *and see* burhs
freeman 22, *and see* Glossary
'Free Miners' 62
furlong (220 yards or eighth of a mile) 41, *and see* Glossary
furs 20, 53, *and see* skins

Gafol land 7, 10, *and see* Glossary
gebur [A–S, tenant, or holder of a yardland, equivalent to villager of Domesday Book] 10, 23, 56, *and see* Glossary
geld, *see* taxation *and* Glossary
geneat [A–S, tenant] 10, 22
geology, *see* soils
grazing (commoning) 63
grindstones 62

haga {A–S], woodland fences 47, *and see* Glossary
haia [A–S], hedged woodland enclosure 45, 48, 75, 82, *and see* Glossary
Halley's comet, AD 989, 76, 77
ham [OE], farm, village, 89, *and see* Glossary
hamm [A–S topographical derivation] 23, *and see* Glossary
hawking and falconry *see* hunting
hedges 25
hide (a measure) 5, 7, 8, 31, *and see* Glossary
hides (for tanning) 20, 25, 39
hillforts 67, Map V; Fig. 21
holloways 6, 59, 67
honey 10, 25, 34, 54
    sester of (32 oz.) 10, 54

horseshoes 56, 62
houses, dwellings 25, 37, 61, 62, 63
household objects, 37, 40, 63
hundreds xiii, 17, 31, 105, Map I, *and see* Glossary *and passim*
    court and meeting-places 17, 85
    in Herefordshire
        Bromsash 91
    in Gloucestershire
        Bledisloe 82, 83, 90
        Botloe 89, 90
        Longbridge 84, 90
        Lydney 83, 84, 90
        St Briavels 62, 90
        Tidenham 83, 90
        Twyford 84, 90
        Westbury 81, 82, 89
hunting, 37, 43–47, 75, 82, 108, 109, 111, *and see* animals, wild; hedged woodland enclosures (*haia*); *and* woodland fences (*haga*); Fig. 10
Hwicce, Anglo-Saxon kingdom of 1, 15, 73
hygiene 52, 61

Ice Age 34
illnesses and remedies 64
industries
    charcoal burning 41
    mining, coal 20
    mining, iron-ore, *see* Index of Place-names
    smelting 41, 61, 62
    smithing 20, 25, 56, 62
    pottery 69
inhabitants 64, 65, *and see* life span, life style, food *and* beverages
    privileges of 63, *and see* buildings, estovers, fencing, firewood *and* grazing (commoning)

Index of Subjects

iron, 20, 56, *and see* smiths
Iron Age 65, 67
iron-ore, mining of, 20, 41, 56, 62, 63, *and see* miners, smiths *and* Index of Place-names; Fig. 15
   forging 61
   smelting of 41, 61, 62
   cinders, uses of 62

Julius Work Calendar 'Labours of the month' (*c.* 1020) 50, 51, 75
   illustrations xviii, 50, 51; Figs 9, 10, 13 and 14
justice 64, 100, 111, *and see* Ordeal *in* Glossary

kingship 74
knowledge, local 59–65
kotsetla [A–S, cottager] 22, 23, *and see* Glossary

landholders by the year 1000, 81–93, 108
   rent of landholdings 81–7
      shillings in 1066 and for 1086, 81–7
      'night's service' (to the shire) 81, 82
      'to go where he would' (free to choose any patron) 82, 85, 86, 110
'landing places' 27, Map V, *and see* ports, 'pills'
land ownership, *see* land tenure
landscape 34–42, 59, 60
land tenure 7, 22, 23, 81, 82, 85, 86
   demesne land (*inland*) 7
language 63
larders, royal, *see* hunting

latrine 61
law and order 64, 100, 111
law
   Cnut's 45
   Æthelred II's, 74, 75, 100
   common 45, 110
   forest, *see* forest law
   royal 44, 45, 111
league (one and a half miles) 41
lēah [A–S], wood-pasture 5, 35, 37, 38, *and see* Glossary
leather 25, *and see* tanning
legislation 100, *and see* law
life span (human) 64
life style 49, 50, 51, 64, 65
lime, as a manure 62
literacy 63
literature, Anglo-Saxon, *see* poetry and riddles
lord (usually of a manor) 22, 29, *and see* Glossary
   allegiance of peasants to 25
   protection of peasants by 25
lynchets 49, *and see* Glossary

Magonsæte, Anglo-Saxon kingdom of 1, 73
manors, manorial 4, 23, 24, *and see* Glossary
manual labour, *see* agriculture *and* slaves
marl, as a manure 62
marriage, intermarriage 23, 33
marshes 42, 59
mast (of oak, beech, and chestnut) 10, 34; Fig. 14
mead, 52
megaliths 65, 66, 67, Map V; Fig. 20
military service, *see* warfare
millennium, the first Christian, 64, 76–7, *and see* Christianity

Index of Subjects

mills, *see* corn mills, water-mills
minsters 25, 63, 72, 73, *and see* churches *and* Glossary
   double 73
mints, minting places, 17, 20, *and see* coinage *and* currency
monasteries, *see* minsters
money, *see* coinage, currency *and* mints
monks 25, *and see* monasteries

nails 56, 62
Navy, *see* ships
Neolithic 34, 65, 69
nets, snares, traps 45, 56
   net-yarn, service of providing 10, 56
Norman Conquest 1066, 65, 81, 101, 105, 111, *and see* castles and camps, Norman, *and* Domesday Book 1086
   Norman Forest of *Dene* 105–11
Normans, 105–11

oath of allegiance to Æthelred II, 64
Offa's Dyke 1, 3, 4, 7, 8, 32, 33, 54, Maps I, II, III and IV; Fig. 1
'open-field' system, *see* agriculture *and* Glossary

paganism 72
pannage [Norman] 10, 34, 40, *and see* mast; Fig. 14
passages (sea) 27, 33, Map III
pasture, *see* wood-pasture, *lēah* [A–S]
peasant 22, 23, 59, *and passim*
   military services, *see* warfare
personal names 63, *and see* Christianity
'pills', *see* ports
plants, helpful 64
ploughmen, ploughteam 49, 81, 83, Fig. 13, *and see* Glossary

poetry, Anglo-Saxon 28, 63
   Beowulf 62, 63
pollarding 39
ponds, pools 59
population 23, 24, 31, 32, 108
ports, 'pills' 26, 27, 37
   on *Sæfern* 26, 27, Map III
   on *Wæge see* Wye
   Welsh, Maps I, II, III and V, *and see* 'landing places'
potatoes 51
pottery 54
pre-1066 information: T.R.E. 81–7, 105, *and see* Glossary
priests 25, 75
privileges, inhabitants *see* inhabitants
punishments, prisons, gallows 64
putcher-weirs, putchers 56–8, 59; Figs 16 and 17

reeve (shire), *see* sheriff
   lord's reeve 12, 24
Region, The xiii, 15, 18, 31, 32, 59, 63, 64, 65, 108, 109, Map I, *and passim*
   Christianity in 72–6
   the first Christian millennium 76, 77
   influence of Wales 32–4, 65
   remoteness 63, 65
   resources 20
   woodland pattern 35, 36
   woodland extent 41, 42
religion, *see* Christianity
riddles, Anglo-Saxon 63
river, *see* Leadon, Monnow, Severn, Usk, Worm, and Wye, *and see* fisheries
river trade 33, 41
tolls of river trade 41

130

Index of Subjects

roads, routeways 17, 26, 30, 59, *and see* holloways
   Roman 4, 7, 26, 62, Maps III and IV
rocks, fallen 70, 71; Fig. 22
Roman period 15, 23, 26, 34, 48, 54, 65, 69, 72
   bridges 26, 69
   dwellings, settlements 15, 23, 24, 48
   roads 4, 7, 26, 69, Maps III, IV and V
   villas 69, Map V

sailors, Welsh 3, 4, 7, 33
saints, saint days, festivals 75
salmon fishing 33, 56, 57; Figs 16 and 17
salt industry 54
sanitation, *see* hygiene
schooling 63
'scowles', old iron-ore workings called 69; Fig. 15
serf, serfdom, 25, 33, *and see* slaves
services, *see* customs
settlements by the year 1000, 81–93, Map VI
settlements subsequent to the year 1000, 94–6, 106, Maps VII and VIII
Severn, *Sæfern* [A–S], *Sauerna* 16, 17, 18, 26, 27 [Norman], 56–8, 59, 60, 61, 90, 105, Maps, Figs 3, 16, 17 and 19, *and passim*
sheriff (shire reeve) 16, 29, 31, 64, *and see* Glossary
ships 37, *and see* tolls
   building 37, 39
   fleets 30, 37
   'long-ships' 28
   ship money 99
   size of ships 37

shire, 15–17, 105, 111, *and see* sheriff *and* Glossary
   court 16
   Gloucester *passim*
   Hereford *passim*
   Winchcombe 15
skins 20, 53, *and see* furs
slaves, *servi* [Norman] 25, 31, 33, 59
smallholder, *see* bordar
smiths 20, 25, 56, 62
soils 4, 48, 62
spectacles 63
springs 24, 59
standard of living 50, 51, 64
stone 62
   grindstones 62
Stone Row 6, 69, Map V; Fig. 2
stones, fallen Map V; Fig. 22
   megaliths Map V; Fig. 22
   placed 6, Map V; Fig. 2
streams 26, 27
'swallow holes', 'swallets' 70

tanning 20, 25, 39
taxation, 17, 19, 20, 22, 28, 30, 31, 50, 64, 82, 99, 108, 110, *and see* tolls, river
   freedom from in *Dene* 82, 110
thegn 22, 47, 74, 82, 87, 88, 100, 105, 110, *and see* Glossary
timber, trade in 33, 36, 41
   use of 35, 37, 39, 40, 41
tithe, church 10, 30, 74, *and see* Glossary
tolls, river 33, 41
tomatoes 51
tools, equipment 25, 62, *and see* agriculture
towns 16, 23, *and see* settlements
trade and commerce 25, 33, 54–56

Index of Subjects

trees, 39, 40, 42, *and see* woodland
  aesthetics 42
  alder 42
  ash 39, 40
  as landmarks 40
  beech 39
  birch 39, 42
  blackthorn 42
  browse-line 38, 39
  cherry 42
  chestnut 39, 42
  hawthorn 39, 40, 42
  hazel 40
  holly 42
  lime 39
  maple (field) 39
  oak 25 (tanbark), 39, 40; Fig. 14
  pollarding 39
  rowan 42
  sallow 39, 42
  service 39
  wych elm 39
  yew 6, 39, 40, 42
tūn, farm, village, *see* Glossary
  bishop's (e.g. Bishton in Tidenham manor) 7
  king's (e.g. Kingston in Tidenham manor and Kingstone in Herefordshire) 87, 92

underwood 41, *and see* coppices

vegetation
  bilberries, wimberries 39, 42, 59
  blackberries 64
  bluebells 42, 59
  bracken 38, 39, 42, 59
  broom 39, 42, 59
  foxglove 42, 59
  gorse 39, 42, 59
  heather 39, 42, 59
  ivy 42
  wild clematis 42
  wild hops 64
venison, *see* deer *and* wild boar
verderers 109
Vikings 19, 23, 28, 29, 30, 64, 99
  place-names 29, 30
  raids 28, 29, 31, 99
villager, *villanus* [Norman; equivalent to the A–S *gebur*] 25, 31, 59, 83, *and see* Glossary
villages, vills 16, 23, *and see* settlements *and* Glossary

Wales and the Welsh 4, 7, 8, 29, 31–4, 54, 65, 72
  Christianity in 72, 76
  influence on The Region 32–4, 65
  land tenures and customs 32
  port 3, 4, 7, Map V
  sailors 3, 4, 7, 90
walls 25
warfare 28, 29, 30, *and see* battles
  hunting as training for 44, 47
  military service 59, 64
  warriors 28, 29, 30; Figs 6, 7 and 8
  weaponry, 28, 29, 30; Figs 6, 7 and 8
warriors, *see* warfare
'waste' 39, 43, 85, 86, 87, 91, 92
water-mills, *see* corn mills
weaving 25
'week work' 12, 23, 56, *and see* Glossary
weirs 10, 56–8, 59
  basket 7, 56, 58
  hackle 7, 56, 58
wells 24
Welsh 3, 4, 31–4, *and see* Wales
  place-names 33, 34
Welshbury Camp 67, Map V

wine, 52
woodland, woods, 24–29, 34–42, Fig. 9, *and see haga* (fences), *haia* (hedged enclosures) *and* coppices
  aesthetics 42
  administration 40
  browse-line 38, 39
  Domesday 1086 measurements of 41, 42
  extent 35, 41, 42
  regeneration 35, 36, 37
  resources 35, 37
wood-pasture (*lēah*) [A–S] 5, 35, 37, 38
  extent 42
wool, trade in 50
Wye, *Wæge* [A–S]; *Waia* [Norman], 26, 27, 32, 33, 56, 58, 59, 61, 90, 94, 95, 105, Maps, Fig. 4, *and passim*

yardland, 7, 8, 23, 25, *and see gebur and* Glossary

INDEX OF PLACE-NAMES

Abenhall 72, 82, 89, 90
Allaston 83
Alton 87, 92
Aluredestone 27, 41, 83, 91, Map V
Alvington 23, 27, 54, 86, 92, 94, Map V
Archenfield (*Ergying* [Welsh], *Ircingafeld* [OE]) 32
Ariconium, Roman town 26, 69, 92, Map V
Arlingham 26
Aston [Ingham] 86, 92
Aust 27, 33, Map III
Avon 16
Avonmouth 30
Awre 23, 30, 54, 82, 90

Aylburton 94

Bath, *Bathum* [A–S] 4, 5, 15, 20, 26, 64, 90
  abbey 4, 5, 8, 12
Beachenhurst 38
Beachley 2, 4, 7, 27, 33, 72, 90, Map IV
Bearse 27, 38
Berkeley 28, 75
Bicknor [English] 23, 27, 39, 82, 89, 105
Bigsweir (on Wye) 27, 49
Bishopswood 27
Bishton 7, 8, 23, 90, Map III
Blaisdon 27, 94

133

Index of Place-Names

Blakeney 27, 94
Bledisloe, Hundred of 58, 82–3, 90
Botloe, Hundred of 84, 85, 91
Braceland 87
Bream 94, iron-ore workings in 54
Brecon Beacons 61
Brierley 27, 94
Broadwell 94
Brockweir (on Wye) 27, 94
Brocote (Lower Redbrook on Wye) 85, 92
Bromsash, Hundred of, in Herefds. xiii, 17, 85, 91
Buckholt 38
Bulley 72, 82, 89

Caerleon-on-Usk (Mon.) 4, 7, 26
Cannop 26, 27, 94
  Chapman's Bridge 26, 94
Chepstow (Mon.) 26, 69, 105, Map IV
  Norman castle (*Striguil*) 26, 69, 84, 105
Churcham, *hamm* 23, 41, 47, 72, 75, 82, 84, 87, 89, 91, 110
Cinderford 24, 26, 27, 39, 94
Cirencester, *Cirenceaster* [A–S] 5, 20, 26, 50, 64
Clearwell 27, 67, 94
Cleeve 54, 58, 86, 92
Coleford 24, 26, 27, 39, 69, 94
Collafield, iron-ore workings in 54
Cone brook 27
Coppitt Hill 18
Corfe (Dorset) 19
Cornwall 19
Cotswolds 50, 61
Cullamore, iron-ore workings in 54
Cumberland, Cumbria 20

Dene; 23, 61, 82, 89, 105, 110, Map V, *and see Magna Dene, Parva Dene, and* Abenhall
Denmark 19, 22, 28
Denny Island 29
Devon 19
Dorset 19
Duni (near Minsterworth) 82
Drybrook 94
Dymock 34, 36, 41, 72, 74, 84, 91
Dyrham (Glouc.) 5

Elton 27
[English] Bicknor, *see* Bicknor
Etloe 58, 83, 90

Flatholm 29
Flaxley 27, 34, 38, 94, Map V
Forest of *Dene*, Dean *passim*

Gloucester, *Gleawanceaster* [A–S]
  Glowecestre [Norman] 4, 5, 7, 17, 26, 28, 51, 54, 56, 59, 61, 64, 105
Gloucestershire, *Gleawanceastsire* [A–S]
  Glowecestscire [Norman] 15, 16, 17, 23, 81–91, Map I
Guscar Rocks 30, Map III
Gwent 32

Hadnock, *Hadenok, Hadenoc, Hodenac* (on Wye) 48, 58, 95
Hagloe 95
Hangerberry 38
Hereford, *Hereford* [A–S] 17, 23, 26, 28, 51, 54, 56, 59, 61, 64
Herefordshire, *Herefordscire* [Norman] 15, 16, 17, 85, 91, 92, Map I
Hewelsfield 27, 43, 72, 84, 91
Highmeadow woods 36, 87

134

Index of Place-Names

Highnam 23, 41, 72, 82, 84, 87, 91
Hope [Long] 23, 27, 59, 61, 82, 89
Hope [Mansell] 86, 92
Howle [Hill] 54, 58, 86, 87, 92
Huntley 23, 36, 41, 59, 85, 91
Huntsham 18, 48, 66, 67, 69, 95; Fig. 20
Hyde, in Newnham 82, 89

Isle of Man 20

Joyford 27

Kent 19
Kingston (Glouc.) 7, 8, 23, 90, Map III
Kingstone (Herefds.) 17, 87, 92

Lambsquay, iron-ore workings in 54
Lancaut (*Land Cawet*) 2, 4, 7, 8, 23, 67, 72, 90, Maps III and IV
Lea 59, 86, 92
Lea Bailey woods 36
Leadon River 73
Linton 86, 92
Littledean, *Parva Dene* 72, 82, 89
Longbridge, Hundred of 82, 84, 91
Longhope *see* Hope [Long]
Lydbrook 27, 95
Lydney 23, 27, 41, 49, 62, 69, 72, 74, 105, Map V
   Hundred of 83, 84, 90, 91
   [Little] Lydney (later St Briavels) 41, 84, 90, 95

Madgett 49, 58, 84, 90, Map IV
Maldon (Essex) 28
Malvern, Forest of 59, 109
May Hill 59, 60, Map V; Fig. 18
Mercia, kingdom of 1, 5, 15, 19, 33, 73

Middleton, Milton 7, 8, 23, 90, Map IV
Minsterworth 72, 82, 89
Mirystock 27, 59
Mitcheldean, *Magna Dene* 39, 72, 82, 89
Monmouth 23, 26, 61, 82
Monmouthshire 72, 74
Monnow River 32
Mork 27, 95
'Morton' 41, 47, 75, 82, 84, 87, 89, 91, 110, Map V

Nass 30, 83, 90
Newent, *Noent* 36, 41, 45, 59, 72, 74, 75, 85, 91
Newland 27, 39, 40, 95
Newnham (on-Severn) 18, 23, 26, 41, 72, 82, 89
Niware, Newerne ('New House') 16, 26, 27, 85, 95
Normandy 19, 99
Noxon, iron-ore workings in 54

Oldbury 27, Maps III and IV

Parkend 27, 95
'Piccadilly' 70, 84
Pillowell 95
Pontshill 86, 92
Poulton 83, 90
Purton 58, 83, 90

Redbrook
   Lower, on Wye (*Brocote*) 23, 27, 43, 85, 92
   Upper 27, 86, 92
Rodley 38, 95
Ross (on-Wye) 36, 72, 74, 87, 92
Ruardean 27, 39, 86, 92

135

Index of Place-Names

Ruddle, near Newnham 82, 83, 89
Ruspidge 24, 26, 27

St Briavels 39, 41, 72, 95, 105
   Hundred of xiii, 62, 90
   origin 72, 90, 95
Scowles, The, west of Coleford, iron-ore workings in 54, 95
Sedbury 3, 7, Maps III and IV
Sharpness 30
Sling 95
Somerset 19
Soudley 27, 95
Speech House 38
Staunton, *Stanton* 23, 27, 43, 54, 70, 71, 86, 87, 92; Fig. 22
Stears, near Newnham 82, 89
Steepholm 29
Stowe 27, 95, 105
Stroat (*Stræt*) 6, 7, 8, 23, 58, 65, 66, 69, 83, 90, Map III
Symonds Yat Rock 61, 67, Map V; Fig. 21

Tallards Marsh 3
Taynton 59, 85, 91
   Little Taynton 85, 91
Tibberton 41, 85, 91
Tidenham (*Dyddanhamme*) 4–8, 12, 23, 32, 33, 41, 56–8, 70, 72, 87, Maps III and IV
   Broad Moor in 6, 7
   Chase, 67, 70, Map V
   customs 8, 10
   Double Ford in 6
   hamlets 7, 23

   Hundred 12, 83, 90
   manor 4–7
   'Parsons allotment' near 70
   White Hollow in 6
Twyford 7, 27
   Hundred of 7, 83, 84, 90

Usk, River 26

Wales 4, 7, 8, 19, 61
   place-names 33, 34
Walford 43, 45, 54, 58, 72, 74, 86, 87, 92
Walmore (Common) 59
Welington, *see* Newland
Westbury (on-Severn) 23, 72, 74, 81
   Hundred of 81, 82, 89
Wessex, kingdom of [A–S] 19
Weston-under-Penyard 17, 26, 69, 86, 92
'Whippington', *Wiboldingtune* [Norman] 43, 58, 87, 92, Map V
   brook 27, 87
Whitecroft 27, 96
Wigpool, iron-ore workings in 54, 59
Wilscroft wood 70
Wilton (Glos.) 54, 58, 86, 92
Winchcombe, the shire of 15
Woolaston 41, 48, 58, 69, 84, 90, 94
Worcester 15, 64
Worm River 32
Wyegate 41, 43, 58, 84, 91
Wyre Forest (Worcs. and Shropshire) 109

Yorkley 96

Index of Personal Names

Ælfgifu of Mercia, first wife of Æthelred II, 19, 99
Aelfric (thegn) 85
Ælfwig, abbot of Bath 12
Æthelred I, king of England 15, 37, 91
Æthelred II, king of England (AD 979–1016) 16, 19–22, 28, 30, 31, 37, 42, 44, 47, 65, 74, 75, 76, 77, 87, 88, 99, 100
   accession (979) 19
   attitude to the first Christian millennium 20, 76, 77
   birth of (c. 968) 19
   coins, coinage, currency of 20, 21; Fig. 5
   died (1016) 99
   escaped to Normandy (1013) 99
   laws of 74, 75, 100
   married Emma of Normandy (1002) 20, 99
   nicknamed 'The Unready' 22, 99
   ordered massacre of all Danes in England (1002) 99
   raids by (1000) 20, 99
   reputation 99, 100
   restoration of (1014) 99
   successors 100
Aldred, archbishop of York 85
Ælfthryth, mother of Æthelred II, 19
Alfred, son of Æthelred II, 19, 99
Alfward (thegn) 85
Alfwold (bishop of Dorset, d. 978) 82
Alric (thegn) 82
Alston, Ælfstan (the great thegn of Boscombe) 84

Alwin, Elfwine, sheriff of Gloucester 82, 84, 85
   wife of 82
Ansger 88
Ansgot (thegn) 86

Bondi, Bundi (? the Constable) 83
Brictric 84, 86
Brictric, Beorhtric, son of Algar, Ælfgar (an important thegn) 84
Brictsi (thegn) 85
Burgred, king of Mercia 91

Ceawlin, king of West Saxons 5
Cnut, king of England 15, 65, 88, 100

Eadred, son of Æthelred II, 19
Eadwig, son of Æthelred II, 19
Eadwig, king of the English 5
Edgar, son of Æthelred II, 19, 101
Edgar, king of the English, father of Æthelred II, 19, 37
Edith dau. of Æthelred II, 19
Edmund II ('Ironside'), king of England 19, 100
Edward the Elder, king of the English 15
Edward the Martyr, king of the English, half-brother of Æthelred II, 19
Edward the Confessor, king of England 12, 17, 45, 58, 65, 81, 85, 86, 99, 100, 101
Edwulf 86

Index of Personal Names

Egbert, son of Æthelred II, 19
Emma of Normandy, Queen,
    wife of Æthelred II, 20, 65, 99
    wife of King Cnut 65, 100
Ernwy (thegn) 82
Ethelred II, *see* Æthelred II

Forne (thegn) 82

Godgifu dau. of Æthelred II, 19, 99
Godric (thegn) 82
Godwine, earl of Wessex, father of
    Earl (King) Harold and Edith
    (wife of King Edward), d. 1053,
    86
Gruffydd, a Welsh King 32
Gunner (*Balistarius*), Walter 86

Hadwic 86
Harold I Harefoot, king of England
    100, 101
Harold II, king of the English 32, 83,
    86, 101
Harthacanut, king of England 100,
    101
Henry III, 63

King John 63

Leofric (earl of Mercia, d. 1057) 86
Leofstan 86

Malcolm, under-king of Cumberland
    20
Morganwy 82

Offa, king of Mercia 1, 4, 5, 16, 33
Osric, prince of Mercia 73

Palli 83

Richard, Duke of Normandy, brother
    of Emma 20, 99

St Alphege 99
St Briavel 72
St Brice 99
St Cewydd 72
St Oswald 73
St Peter 73
St Techychius 72
Siward, Siweard (the Danish earl of
    Northumbria, d. 1055) 83
Stigand, archbishop of Canterbury 8,
    12, 83
Sweyn Forkbeard, king of Denmark
    and of England 99

Taldus 86
Tovi the Proud (thegn) 82, 88

Wihenoc (Lord of Monmouth) 82
William, Earl of Hereford 12
William I, the Conqueror, king of
    England 105–11
Winstan 83
Wulfheah (thegn, blinded 1016) 82, 84
Wulfhild 19
Wulfnoth (thegn of Wessex) 84
Wulfgar, abbot of Bath 5
Wulfgar (thegn) 85